RESTO A GO-GO

**180 cheap and
fun places
to eat and drink
in Montreal**

Sarah Musgrave

Published by ECW PRESS
2120 Queen Street East, Suite 200, Toronto, Ontario, Canada M4E 1E2

NATIONAL LIBRARY OF CANADA CATALOGUING IN PUBLICATION DATA

Musgrave, Sarah
Resto à go-go: 180 cheap and fun places to eat and drink
in Montreal / Sarah Musgrave.

Includes index.
ISBN 1-55022-560-X

1. Restaurants—Quebec (Province)—Montréal—Guidebooks.
2. Bars (Drinking establishments)—Quebec (Province)—Montréal—
Guidebooks. 3. Montréal (Quebec)—Guidebooks. I. Title.

TX907.5.C22M6 2003   647.95714'28   C2002-905419-2

Acquisition editors: Elizabeth Walker & Emma McKay
Copy editor: Mary Williams
Interior design: Guylaine Régimbald—Solo Design
Typesetting: Yolande Martel
Production: Emma McKay
Printing: Transcontinental
Cover design: Joel Shane—Graphic Material

This book is set in Franklin Gothic

The publication of *Resto à Go-Go: 180 Cheap and Fun Places to Eat
and Drink in Montreal* has been generously supported by the Canada
Council, by the Government of Ontario through the Ontario Media
Development Corporation's Ontario Book Initiative, by the Ontario
Arts Council, and by the Government of Canada through the Book
Publishing Industry Development Program. Canada

DISTRIBUTION

CANADA: Jaguar Book Group, 100 Armstrong Avenue,
Georgetown, Ontario L7G 5S4

UNITED STATES: Independent Publishers Group,
814 North Franklin Street, Chicago, Illinois 60610

PRINTED AND BOUND IN CANADA

ECW PRESS
ecwpress.com

This book is dedicated to anyone who finds that food tastes just a little better when you're getting a deal on it.

Contents

INTRODUCTION

EATING

Breakfast Binge

Late-Night Eats

Vegging Out

Meat and Potatoes

Grills and Gills

Out of Africa

Novelty Nosh

On the Run

Something Sweet

DRINKING

Introduction

Resto À Go-Go is designed to help you get the most out of this city for the least amount of money. It's a comprehensive guide to the best of Montreal's food and drink for people on a budget, with reviews of 140 restaurants where you can eat for $15 or less, along with 42 bars where you can take in the nightlife.

A whole lot of research, mostly in the form of thoroughly enjoyable eating and imbibing, went into the making of this book. Montreal has been scoured from the east end to the West Island, and the search has yielded all sorts of ethnic edibles—like Brazilian breakfasts, Jamaican jerk chicken, authentic Israeli falafel, and Korean tabletop barbecue. In these pages, you'll discover Egyptian sheesha smokers, Italian ice cream emporiums, aromatic Afghani appetizers, and the best pierogi this side of Poland. Along the way, you'll find some truly memorable meals in some extraordinary restaurants—like the place that fines you if you don't finish your plate, an international water cellar, and a kitschy Polynesian buffet. This book will also point you in the direction of some of the latest culinary trends: bento-box lunches from Japan; bubble tea from Taiwan; and pupusas, the hottest street food from Latin America.

The list of bars in the nightlife section reflects a cross-section of Montreal after dark. Listings include the best brewpubs, outdoor terraces, and cocktail hours the city has to offer. Among them: the brasserie that supplies beer to the Czech consulate, a club where a drag queen hosts karaoke soirées, hidden rooftop patios, upscale whisky lounges, and pubs that serve good grub to soak it all up.

About This Book

All of the restaurants in these pages are fun and affordable. Affordable, in the sense that at any of them you can eat well for $15 or less. You should be able to order any of the menu items, and even the table d'hôte, for that price (before taxes, tip, and drinks). In fact, in many cases, it would be hard to spend more than $15 if you tried! However, this guide does cover a few eateries where, though you'll be offered excellent value, you may have to exercise a little restraint to stay within that limit. As for the fun, that comes from sampling the richly diverse cuisines that make this city so exciting.

The restaurants are divided into 20 categories, with 7 entries in each. They're classified according to cravings and convenience. If you need a sugar fix, you'll want to check out Something Sweet. If your stomach is rumbling at 2 a.m., head to Late-Night Eats. And if you don't have time for a sit-down dinner, On the Run is your ticket to a takeout meal.

At the back of the book, you'll find three indexes for easy reference—alphabetical, by area, and by cuisine—so that you won't overlook a place that specializes in Peruvian breakfasts when you're on a search for a South American eatery. *Resto À Go-Go* also features bite-size summaries and up-to-date listings, including opening hours, directions, alcohol availability, wheelchair access, and vegetarian friendliness.

You won't find big chain restaurants here, and no establishment has paid in any way, shape, or form to be listed in these pages. All reviews were conducted independently, without the prior knowledge of restaurant management.

About the Author

Intrepid food reporter Sarah Musgrave is the casual dining critic for the Montreal *Gazette*, the city's daily newspaper. She was previously the managing editor and restaurant reviewer for the *Mirror*, the city's leading English-language alternative news and entertainment weekly.

Byblos

Start your day with the faraway flavours of Persia.

A morning sojourn at Byblos is like taking a mini-vacation in a foreign land. This Persian café occupies an airy space, and its whitewashed walls, large windows, and Oriental embroideries provide a backdrop for some of the most subtle tastes and textures of the Middle East.

Although it's popular at any hour, breakfast is definitely Byblos's most unique feature. In Iran, the morning meal is called sobhaneh, and it's dramatically different from the bacon and eggs experience. It usually includes sweet tea, cheese, and bread, along with a vast array of marmalade concoctions in fanciful flavours like ginger-pineapple or orange blossom.

The omelettes are more like smooth, creamy scrambled eggs, laid out in a thin layer on the plate. The Oriental is made with flour, sugar, rose petals, and cardamom, for a cleansing, perfumed effect. The Feta omelette is intense and savoury, with a liberal sprinkling of fresh herbs. All are served with a basket of flatbreads and a choice of marmalade, as well as coffee, tea, hot chocolate, or a small juice ($6.90). The Mixed Breakfast Plate ($6.50) includes soft Feta cheese, olives, walnuts, almonds, halvah studded with pistachios, and a bouquet of herbs. Another option for the adventurous is halym, a blend of cream of wheat, cinnamon, sugar, and . . . turkey!

Hours: Tues.–Sun. 9 a.m.–11 p.m.
Alcohol: Yes
Credit cards: Yes
Wheelchair access: Yes
Vegetarian friendly: Yes

1499 Laurier E. (@ Fabre)
(514) 523-9396
Metro: Laurier, 27 bus

Chez Clo

A Québécois breakfast fit for a lumberjack.

Chez Clo dishes up old-time Québécois breakfasts, the kind lumberjacks fortified themselves with before heading into the bush. Settle down with a copy of the *Journal de Montréal*, order a coffee from the quirky wait staff, and you're all set for a complete immersion into east-end culture. This large diner, with several bright rooms and a terrace, is located in the blue-collar Hochelaga-Maisonneuve district, kitty-corner to the eye-catching Nativité-de-la-Sainte-Vierge church.

For a mere $3.10, the Chez Clo breakfast includes two eggs, home-fried potatoes, toast, and three kinds of meat: sausage, bacon, and ham. Add 35 cents for a side order of fèves au lard—sweet, home-baked brown beans. Several omelettes are available during the week, but on weekends the selection is more limited. Instead, featured dishes might include eggs Benedict, strangely served atop a pancake and accompanied by a tasty potato mash and loads of fresh fruit.

For lunch and dinner, there's plenty of down-home cooking for well under $10. Expect food like maman used to make: meatloaf, liver and onions, and creton (a chunky pâté). Chez Clo is also famous for its tourtière, both the homestyle version with ground beef and the deep-dish Saguenay version with cubed meat and potatoes. A large pie will easily feed a family of 10 for $25.

Hours: 6 a.m.–10 p.m. daily
Alcohol: Yes
Credit cards: No
Wheelchair access: Through terrace
Vegetarian friendly: No

3199 Ontario E. (@ Dézéry)
(514) 522-5348
Metro: Préfontaine

Cosmo

Take the cholesterol challenge at this distinctive diner.

For more than 30 years, Cosmo has been putting the "grease" in greasy spoon. This tiny neighbourhood diner seems to exist in a magical time and place where the ill effects of cholesterol have yet to be discovered. It's so legendary that the owner was immortalized in a documentary film, appropriately titled *Man of Grease*. Tony Koulakis has recently retired, turning the enterprise over to his children. They continue to work the grill, whipping up delicious, man-sized breakfasts.

A popular order here is the Creation ($4.75), a breakfast sandwich filled with fried egg, bacon, salami, cheese, lettuce, and tomato. It's made with any number of breads, including rye, pumpernickel, bagel, whole wheat, or challah. But the accompanying hash browns, potatoes and onions scraped off the grill in a crusty yet soft mass, are the real pièce de résistance.

Regular breakfasts cost less than $5. That will buy you a generous plate of two eggs, a choice of meat, toast, and a clump of those heavenly hash browns. Also look for the Good Morning Cheeseburger, topped with bacon and a fried egg. But for the real Cosmo challenge, don't miss the Mish-Mash Special, an omelette that contains no fewer than four eggs, onions, tomatoes, and cheese, along with just about every meat imaginable. Share a double with your friend or neighbour for $6 each.

Hours: Tues.–Sun. 7 a.m.–5 p.m.
Alcohol: No
Credit cards: No
Wheelchair access: Sidewalk terrace only
Vegetarian friendly: Yes

5843 Sherbrooke W. (@ Draper)
(514) 486-3814
Metro: Vendôme, 105 bus

Dustys

Old classics for a young crowd.

Just a stone's throw from the lush greenery of Mount Royal, Dustys has been in the breakfast business since 1949. Its recent expansion—including a new and improved terrace—was met with sighs of relief from legions of fans who often had to endure long lineups. And for good reason: for a sociable budget breakfast on the Plateau, this place is hard to beat.

People are likely to linger here, thanks in part to the bottomless cups of coffee, continually refilled by a bevy of buxom waitresses. The breakfast special—served all day, every day—includes three eggs served any way you want, home fries, and a choice of sausage, bacon, or ham. The special also comes with toast (white, brown, or bagel), coffee, and a glass of orange juice. It will set you back $3.95, $4.95, or $5.95, depending on the size of juice you choose.

In addition to French toast and pancakes, the slightly sweet and creamy homemade cheese blintzes with sour cream and blueberry sauce ($6.50) are worth a try. For the same price, the bagel burger of cream cheese, smoked salmon, and onions makes a good hold-in-your-hand meal. There are also real burgers on the lunch menu, along with other diner standards.

Hours: 7 a.m.–7 p.m. daily
Alcohol: No
Credit cards: No
Wheelchair access: No
Vegetarian friendly: Yes

4510 du Parc (@ Mont-Royal)
(514) 276-8525
Metro: Mont-Royal, 97 bus/Place-des-Arts, 80 bus

Melchorita

Peruvian desayunos that stick to your ribs.

Melchorita's whopping breakfasts seem to be imported directly from Peru—as do many of its customers. On weekends, this unassuming spot fills up with South American families, who hunker down over communal plates of authentic desayunos peruanos. Designed to be shared, the Desayuno Familiar is $11.95, or $7.95 for a half-order (enough for two). The focus of the platter is meat, in the form of tasty chicharron, a satisfyingly chewy pork roast, and slices of relleno, a dark, salty sausage. You also get a corn-flour tamale, stuffed with hard-boiled egg, green olives, pork rind, and yellow peas, along with a heaping portion of camote—freshly fried sweet-potato chips. This selection is accompanied by Spanish onions sprinkled with hot peppers. A second breakfast special ($9.95 for two) exchanges the tamale for an empanada with a beef, chicken, or vegetable filling ($2.95 ordered separately, with salad). Wash it all down with Chanchamayo coffee or chicha morada, a purple corn drink that dates back to Incan times.

After breakfast, the kitchen turns its attention to regional dishes, which Melchorita offers at remarkably reasonable prices. A whole pollo a la brasa, chicken roasted in-house, can feed four for $17.95 (with fries and salad). Other entrées are priced under $10, with the exception of some seafood specialties.

Hours: Mon.–Fri. 8:30 a.m.–10 p.m.; Sat. and Sun. 8:30 a.m.–11 p.m.
Alcohol: Yes
Credit cards: Yes
Wheelchair access: One step
Vegetarian friendly: No

7901 St-Dominique (@ Gounod)
(514) 382-2129
Metro: de Castelnau or Jarry

Place Milton

Cheerful breakfasts at student-friendly prices.

Place Milton must rival the university library as the place most frequented by McGill students. But anyone will feel welcome here—the staff is affectionate and funny, often pausing, coffee-pot in hand, to chat with customers. The kitchen area pays homage to the place's hole-in-the-wall past, while the bright, cheery dining room and the covered rear terrace make it cozy even on a rainy day.

The Place Milton Special is a great deal if you're really and truly hungry. It includes three eggs, two crêpes, ham, sausage, and bacon for $6.49. Other breakfasts (about $3.50 each) are loosely named for their country of origin. The American offers two eggs with ground beef, the Germanic comes with sausages. With the Ménage à Trois, three kinds of meat love it up on your plate. Add a heaping portion of fruit to your order for $1.99 extra, or opt for a choice of fresh fruit juices—like kiwi, blueberry, banana, cantaloupe, pineapple, honeydew melon, or mango.

Place Milton boasts "breakfasts and more." The more is mostly burgers—beef, chicken, and vegetarian—along with a few daily specials like a Brie and ham omelette or Caesar salad with grilled chicken. At less than $7 each, these full meals—including soup, dessert, and coffee—are a good deal.

Hours: Mon.–Fri. 7 a.m.–5 p.m.; Sat. and Sun. 8 a.m.–5 p.m.
Alcohol: No
Credit cards: No
Wheelchair access: One step
Vegetarian friendly: Yes

220 Milton (@ Jeanne-Mance)
(514) 285-0011
Metro: Place-des-Arts

Senzala

Inventive brunches with Brazilian sizzle.

Ever wonder what Brazilians eat for breakfast? You'll find the answer to that question and more on your plate at Senzala, a Mile End restaurant that serves up an exotic weekend brunch.

Among the more unusual dishes is the Tropicana ($8.50): two poached eggs in a sliced-open avocado or mango, gratinéed, drizzled with tomato sauce, and served with bacon, sausage, or ham. This dish is rivalled only by the Contessa ($8.50): eggs on an English muffin, topped with sauce, artichoke hearts, and crumbled blue cheese. These specialties come with fried plantain, hash browns, and, best of all, hot-off-the-grill fruit brochettes on metal skewers. The omelettes also have a tropical twist, including the Mediterraneo, with Feta, vine leaves, and olives. For an eggless meal, try the Bom Dia ($9.95), a plate of grilled Brie, toasted almonds, and fresh fruit.

During the summer, it gets as hot as Bahía inside Senzala, but there's a mini-terrace where you can catch a breeze. Alternately, cool off with a batida, a smooth, blenderized drink of coconut milk, condensed milk, and cachaça.

Senzala is also open for dinner, offering Brazilian staples at decent prices. These include fish stews, steaks, and feijoada, a traditional dish of beef, pork, black beans, and garlic. Live music midweek adds to the atmosphere.

Hours: Mon.–Wed. 5 p.m.–10 p.m.; Thurs.–Sun. 9 a.m.–3 p.m., 5 p.m.–10 p.m.
Alcohol: Yes
Credit cards: Yes
Wheelchair access: One step
Vegetarian friendly: Yes

---

177 Bernard W. (@ Esplanade)
(514) 274-1464
Metro: Outremont, 161 bus/St-Laurent, 55 bus

EATING
late-night eats

Angela Pizzeria

Heart-warming pizzas for a cold night.

When a 99-cent slice just won't cut it, come to this pizzeria for the kind of substantial pie that fits the bill. The crust is thick, crisp, and satisfying, and Angela doesn't hold back on the toppings. All-Dressed seems like diet food when you compare it with the ingredients of the Angela Special: bacon, onions, tomatoes, mushrooms, green pepper, and pepperoni. The Greek version is almost gourmet, topped with onion, tomato, Feta cheese, and Kalamata olives. Pizzas start at $7.30 for a 10-inch and rise to $16.75 for an extra-large.

While pizza has garnered Angela most of its fans, the rest of the menu is a happy marriage between Greek and Italian fare, so much so that you'd think those two national cuisines actually originated in the Land of the Late-Night Snacks. All the standard pastas can be had for under $10. Souvlaki plates served with rice, fries, and salad are similarly priced, as are the barbecued quarter-chicken and the pikilia platter of tzatziki, taramasolata, spinach pie, stuffed vine leaves, Feta, and olives. The grilled chicken burger ($5.25), made with a breast charred on the grill, is also very tasty. With just about any choice, the output from the kitchen is consistent. The décor is decent enough to eat in, but Angela does provide takeout and delivery service.

Hours: 11 a.m.–5 a.m. daily
Alcohol: Yes
Credit cards: Yes
Wheelchair access: No
Vegetarian friendly: Yes

1662 de Maisonneuve W. (@ St-Marc)
(514) 933-2000
Metro: Guy-Concordia

Arahova

Souvlaki that will really take your breath away.

For many Montrealers, Arahova is the last stop after last call. Now, with added locations downtown and on the West Island (301 Brunswick, Pointe-Claire), what started as a Mile End family restaurant has become even more popular for the Greek delights it serves in the middle of the night.

This establishment does a brisk trade in souvlaki ($3.95). That's due in no small part to the wonderfully creamy, dense tzatziki that doesn't stint on the garlic—perfect if you're resigned to sleeping solo or if your date wants to share your potent breath as the sun comes up. Pita sandwiches are available with chicken, pork, or vegetarian fillings; this last is particularly good for its contrast of rich Feta cheese with fresh cukes and tomatoes.

Another popular cheap pick here is the savoury sliced gyro, especially the newer chicken version, presented as a burger ($4.45). For something more substantial, order homemade lentil soup and follow it up with another Greek staple like skordalia, taramosalata, or spanakopita. Home-cooked meals like pasticcio, moussaka, or dolmades with lemon-egg sauce are pricier, at around $13. Try the galaktoboureko for dessert, a firm custard square topped with honey-infused filo dough.

Hours: Mon.–Thurs. 10:30 a.m.–2 a.m.; Fri. and Sat. 10:30 a.m.–5 a.m.
Alcohol: Yes
Credit cards: Yes
Wheelchair access: No
Vegetarian friendly: Yes

1425 Crescent
(@ Ste-Catherine)
(514) 499-0262
Metro: Peel

256 St-Viateur W.
(@ Jeanne-Mance)
(514) 274-7828
Metro: Place-des-Arts, 80 bus

La Banquise

Redefining the diner, girl-style.

Cute all-grrrrl staff, good tunes, and free newspapers make this casse-croûte, located few steps away from Park Lafontaine and the St-Denis strip, a welcoming late-night spot. With its multi-coloured walls and hand-painted tabletops, it's a vast improvement over the dreary diner that once occupied this space. In summer, there's a tiny terrace out back where you can refresh your lungs after a night in a smoky bar.

Comfort food is the specialty of the house. There are 15 kinds of poutine on offer, ranging in price from $3.91 for the regular size to $7.45 for a truly enormous portion. They run the gamut from Italian to veggie to a three-meat extravaganza. The Elvis (undoubtedly inspired by his later period) is made with ground beef, mushrooms, and fried peppers. The Olé Olé features Italian sausage, hot peppers, and Tabasco.

La Banquise also serves several variations on the hotdog, including steamed, roasted, cheese, bacon, Michigan, and, of course, the batter-encrusted pogo with mustard on the side. If you're with a date, get the club sandwich for two, which comes with a double dose of fries and coleslaw for under 10 bucks. Daily meal specials, which include soup, dessert, and coffee, go for about $6.50. You can cut through the greasy goodness with your choice of microbrewery products.

Hours: 24/7
Alcohol: Yes
Credit cards: No; Interac accepted
Wheelchair access: Through rear terrace
Vegetarian friendly: Yes

994 Rachel E. (@ Mentana)
(514) 525-2415
Metro: Sherbrooke

Chez Claudette

Old-school Plateau snackbar.

In the great debate over who invented poutine, Chez Claudette likes to make its voice heard. It offers this gooey snack of cheese curds, fries, and gravy with just about any meal—including its all-day, all-night breakfast—for a small extra charge. The melted mess takes on a special hue in the restaurant's neon-lit interior. If you want to make a meal of poutine alone, try the Galvaude ($6.50 or $7.75), made with chicken and peas, or the Dalton, which adds smoked sausage to the mix.

Chez Claudette's breakfast specials, featuring eggs, meat, and grilled potatoes, start at $3.50, rising a little in price for extras like Polish sausage. Omelettes of every variety in the spectrum range from $3.75 to $6.25. The Steak Matin ($10), served with two eggs, might be named for the morning, but it will fill you up anytime.

This resto caters to vegetarians, offering grilled or steamed tofu dogs, a meatless club sandwich, and veggie poutine (as long as you can overlook the brown sauce). The rest of the menu is pretty much what you'd expect from a French Canadian food emporium: fish and chips, liver and onions, and salmon pie. The Clau Burger is a little more inventive—it's comprised of two kinds of meat, white cheese, tomato, lettuce, and salsa and sells for $4.95.

Hours: 24/7
Alcohol: Yes
Credit cards: Mastercard, Visa
Wheelchair access: Two steps
Vegetarian friendly: Yes

351 Laurier E. (@ Drolet)
(514) 279-5173
Metro: Laurier

Le Club Sandwich

Clubs for the postclub crowd in a fifties environment.

This Gay Village hangout has long been popular as an after-hours spot, catering to clubbers from the Ste-Catherine strip and further afield. It's part of the enormous Complexe Bourbon, which encompasses a hotel, multilevel patios, and a baffling array of dining areas. With its chrome siding and rounded windows, Le Club Sandwich stands out from its neighbours. Behind those windows are coveted booth seats, ideally positioned for people-watching as the hard bodies emerge from nearby gyms. The resto's interior is full of retro memorabilia—fifties jukeboxes, taxi meters, and old-style diner booths—with a cutesy menu to match.

As the name would suggest, there are lots of club sandwiches to choose from here—no less than 22 variations ($8.95 for one person, $16.80 for two, including fries, dill pickle, and coleslaw). These double-decker creations are offered with turkey, roast pork, tuna, eggs and ham, or spicy German sausage. The meatless club is made with veggie pâté, Swiss cheese, alfalfa sprouts, lettuce, and tomatoes. The burgers are named after old cars, like the Studebaker and the Thunderbird. The Rolls Royce is one of the best—a thick patty on a sesame bun with cream cheese, bacon, and onions ($7.35). The portions here are suited to the place's all-American diner esthetic: they're huge!

Hours: 24/7
Alcohol: Yes
Credit cards: Yes
Wheelchair access: Yes
Vegetarian friendly: Yes

1270 Ste-Catherine E. (@ Champlain)
(514) 523-4679
Metro: Papineau

Keung Kee

Copious portions of Cantonese classics and delicacies.

Chinatown is a good destination for a late-night meal, because you'll always find at least one or two of its restaurants hopping into the wee hours. The second-storey Keung Kee may not be the last to close, but it's one of the more welcoming establishments in the area. Great for groups, it's got an upbeat atmosphere and often remains crowded until closing time.

There's a huge selection of freshly cooked dishes on the menu, so you're sure to satisfy your Cantonese cravings. Main courses range from $6 to $12. For a great combination of tastes and textures, try the steamed half-chicken with smoked sausage and nutty Chinese mushrooms. The deep-fried tofu is also good: puffed bean curd pockets that are golden on the outside and soft on the inside, served atop greens studded with fresh garlic. Most of the simple vegetable dishes, like the Yu Hsiang eggplant, are healthy and tasty. Meals end with fresh oranges and fortune cookies.

In addition to copious Chinese standards, there are unusual items to be had at Keung Kee. These include delicacies, like shark's fin soup and bird's nest soup, that will set you back a pretty penny—up to $80 a bowl.

Hours: 11:30 a.m.–2 a.m. daily
Alcohol: Yes
Credit cards: Yes
Wheelchair access: No
Vegetarian friendly: Yes

---

70 de la Gauchetière W., second floor (@ Clark)
(514) 393-1668
Metro: Place-d'Armes

New Tripolis

A piece of Greece without the grease.

This Greek restaurant is a paradise for anyone who's spent pre-dawn hours working hard, whether it be sweating it out on the night shift or on the dance floor. It provides the kind of freshly cooked full meals you'd think would only be available during regular dining hours.

Fish, seafood, and marinated meats are on display behind a glass-fronted counter near the open kitchen. Calamari, whole red snapper, whiting, and sardines await, and they all look like they've recently come from the fishmonger next door. Take your pick, and the cook will fry it up for you in a heavy pan on his primitive gas range.

A marinated chicken breast or a large serving of sliced Greek sausage, called loukaniko, with salad and potatoes will set you back $12. Lamb chops are $14, veal is $12, and pork souvlaki plates start at $7.50. Meals come with an enormous salad, but it's worth the loonie to upgrade to a "village" version, with lots of crumbled Feta.

The pikilia plate, a mix of delicious dips and salads served with thick, crusty bread, is immensely satisfying. Other real Greek treats to look out for include avgholemono soup ($6.50), which unfurls a blend citrus and chicken on your tongue, and saganaki ($10), fried Kefalotiri cheese that's insanely salty but strangely satisfying.

Hours: 24/7
Alcohol: Yes
Credit cards: Yes
Wheelchair access: No
Vegetarian friendly: No

679 St-Roch (@ Bloomfield)
(514) 277-4689
Metro: Parc

EATING
vegging out

Café Les Entretiens

A warehouse of earthy and earthly delights.

This café feels like an old warehouse in France, with its lofty ceilings, creaky wooden floors, and church-pew seating. There's always a great lineup of daily specials, most of which are vegetarian ($9.95 to $13.95, including appetizer and beverage; subtract $2 without). Meals begin with a choice of vegetable soups and salads, such as red cabbage coleslaw with cumin, or asparagus in vinaigrette. The eight or so main courses might include tourtière made with seitan or millet, a melted mound of Swiss raclette, or pasta with Brie and sun-dried tomatoes.

The warm chèvre salad from the regular menu is a delight of goat cheese croutons, mesclun, walnuts, and apples sprinkled with raspberry vinaigrette. Other salads—Caesar, Greek, Niçoise, and Anglaise (with sharp Cheddar, hard-boiled egg, and cucumber)—are offered with an array of dressings, including garlic, apple, and tamari. In the sandwich section, the top man is the croque-monsieur with tuna, thyme, and a tapenade of anchovies, olives, and garlic ($5.75).

Breakfasts here are also a healthy and happy experience. Even lowly oatmeal is transformed into a treat, with milk, hazelnuts, and raisins, or pear juice, almonds, and yogurt. Tisanes and tempting fruit shakes further encourage you to lose track of time and place, and you'll return to the street the better for it.

Hours: 9 a.m.–11 p.m. daily
Alcohol: Yes
Credit cards: Yes
Wheelchair access: One step

1577 Laurier E. (@ Fabre)
(514) 521-2934
Metro: Laurier, 27 bus/Papineau, 45 bus

Govinda Jaya Jaya

Vegan/vegetarian buffet in serene surroundings.

This is a wonderful place to indulge in a carefully constructed, all-you-can-eat vegetarian buffet. Light filters in through the large windows, bathing the room in an orange-gold glow. A strictly non-smoking, nondrinking environment, Govinda exudes tranquility, maybe because it's run by Hare Krishnas—although other than the artwork, there's almost no hint of religious affiliation here.

The buffet costs $6.95 at lunch and $8.95 in the evening. There's a choice of two daily soups, one of which is usually a comforting lentil dal that tastes even better accompanied by a crackling pappadam. Before loading up on the hot offerings, you can build yourself a fresh, crunchy salad and drizzle it with a vinaigrette or tahini dressing.

The preparations in the hot trays change daily, and nondairy selections are identified for those on restricted diets. Offerings include Thai, Indian, and Mediterranean fare, such as eggplant Parmesan, potato and cauliflower curry, and kofta balls made with chickpea flour, cabbage, and carrot in a light, tangy tomato sauce. There are also delicious red and green peppers stuffed with a savoury rice concoction. The organic tofu is cooked alternately in a creamy peanut-butter sauce or with vegetables and coconut milk. Desserts include carob brownies and baklava. Delivery and catering are also available.

Hours: Sun.–Thurs. 11:30 a.m.–9:30 p.m.; Fri. and Sat. 11:30 a.m.–10:30 p.m.
Alcohol: No
Credit cards: All except Mastercard
Wheelchair access: No

263 Duluth E. (@ Laval)
(514) 284-5255
Metro: Mont-Royal

Lola Rosa

Latino lite.

Drenched in pastel pinks and greens, Lola Rosa looks like a throwback to the days of *Miami Vice*, except it's more like Miami Nice: here you'll find all sorts of good, healthy things under one roof. Just a stone's throw from the McGill campus, it's an oasis of vegetarian food, plants, and mellow music. Dishes are affordably priced at $7.50 to $9.50.

In keeping with the tropical theme, the menu looks south for inspiration: avocado quesadillas, veggie chili, meatless tacos, and a black bean burrito—a huge tortilla folded over a clove-scented mixture, topped with sour cream, and served with rice or salad. For something more earthy, try the hemp burger, which is concocted of hemp seeds, lentils, and veggies, with a hint of curry. It's so mushy that it's hard to eat, but it's surprisingly good. The burger is served on a bagel, and it comes with a substantial salad of lettuce, carrots, and beets. Other meals include a four-cheese lasagne, polenta with ratatouille, and the Rosa Salad with Feta, olives, vegetables, and fruit.

Alcoholic beverages are not available, but you can order a bottle of red or rosé Amé, a sparkling drink made with fruit juice, ginseng, jasmine, lime flowers, and other ingredients that will give your body a break. And for dessert: coffee and vegan chocolate cake.

Hours: Mon.–Fri. 11:30 a.m.–8 p.m.
Alcohol: No
Credit cards: No
Wheelchair access: Yes

---

545 Milton (@ Aylmer)
(514) 287-9337
Metro: McGill

Nu Art Café

Neighbourhood resto with arty, hearty fare.

This is the kind of comfortable, quirky place that every neighbourhood should have. Brick walls, copper-topped tables, and leopard prints set the mood for inventive, healthy food, affordably priced at about $7 to $10 per dish.

Nu Art's salads, which grace just about every plate, are a real standout. Far from being merely a bunch of space-filling greens, they're handcrafted, combining fluffy lettuce with veggies and cubes of mango, cantaloupe, and strawberry in a light balsamic dressing. Sandwiches are also special, like the Chagall—marinated eggplant, goat cheese, and olives served on a bagel; or the Aznavour—pesto, Feta, tomato, olives, and sun-dried tomatoes on a baguette.

To taste an array of house specialties, order the Composition, a mixed plate featuring a savoury spinach terrine, lightly curried homemade veggie pâté, and a hunk of Brie, served with salsa, pesto, and a scoop of distinctively nutty hummus. The rest of the menu showcases more hearty, healthy stuff, like the Zen Veggie Burger, the Piaf Ratatouille, and the Babouchka, a burrito roll filled with a seasoned lentil mixture. Under the heading "Less Vegetarian," tacked onto the end of the menu, you'll find two meat plates.

Hours: Wed. and Thurs. 11:30 a.m.–midnight;
Fri. 11 a.m.–10 p.m.; Sat. 10 a.m.–10 p.m.;
Sun. 10 a.m.–3 p.m. (breakfast only)
Alcohol: Yes
Credit cards: No
Wheelchair access: No

3780 Wellington (@ Regina)
(514) 762-1310
Metro: de l'Église

Pushap Sweets

Indian eatery where the spice and the price are right.

There's enough selection and spice at this no-frills Indian restaurant to delight vegetarians while distracting carnivores from the absence of meat. And since most dishes cost less than $4, there's no question that you can feast to your heart's content. As you dig into various plates, you'll soon notice one of the most remarkable things about Pushap: the spicing of each dish is distinct from the next—a sure sign that items are prepared individually.

For maximum sampling at a minimum price, the Thali Special ($4.95 or $5.95) is the way to go. Each section of a metal platter is filled with a different element of the meal, including two vegetable curries of the day, chickpea or lentil purée, rice, and a choice of breads. For simmered veggies you might be served zucchini, eggplant, cauliflower, okra, or a yummy potato and yam curry called alu zimikand. The dal tarka is divine—yellow lentils simmered with spices and bits of browned onion and garlic. Curries and various paneer dishes with cheese can be ordered separately. There are several kinds of bread on offer, but the fluffy, nanlike bhatura is the best for scooping up sauce. Pushap doubles as a bakery, so be sure to finish up with a spice tea and a pastry.

Hours: 11 a.m.–9 p.m. daily
Alcohol: No
Credit cards: No
Wheelchair access: Yes

5195 Paré	**4777 des Sources, Pierrefonds**
(@ Mountain Sights)	**(@ Pierrefonds)**
(514) 737-4527	**(514) 683-0105**
Metro: Namur	**Metro: Du Collège, 214 bus**

Spirite Lounge

A memorable evening at the intersection of granola and gourmet.

This eclectic Gay Village eatery, its windows lined with glittery tinfoil and Christmas lights, draws veg-heads from far and wide. A night here promises to be unforgettable, especially if you don't finish all of the food on your plate. If you don't, you'll be expected to pay a small fine that will be donated to charity. It's all part of the socially and environmentally conscious esthetic of the place.

The same original thinking has gone into designing the menu, which puts a premium on organic and vegan-friendly ingredients. The food, like the décor and the flamboyant host's outfits, is highly inventive. There's no printed menu here; instead, your waiter will reel off a detailed description of the day's choices. The starter might be soup, a spring roll, a warm spinach salad with apple-cider vinaigrette, or roasted garlic and mushrooms. The main dish is built around a hot crêpe with a legume-based filling, topped with sauce and a scoop of sumptuous, melting sorbet. Desserts, like the triple chocolate bread, are sweetened with fruit, not sugar.

Although prices have gone up, Spirite remains relatively afford-able—a main course and an appetizer will set you back $12.75. An open mind and reservations are essential.

Hours: Sun.–Wed. 5 p.m.–10 p.m.; Thurs. 5 p.m.–11 p.m.; Fri. and Sat. 5 p.m.–midnight
Alcohol: Yes
Credit cards: Yes
Wheelchair access: Yes

1205 Ontario E. (@ Montcalm)
(514) 522-5353
Metro: Beaudry or Berri-UQAM

Les Vivres

A global village of vegan delights.

The food at Les Vivres is as creative and free-flowing as the space itself. Hidden away on a residential Plateau side street, the establishment is a maze of rooms that open onto a charming terrace surrounded by trees. This is vegetarianism at its most dedicated, and the regulars are better described as followers than customers. The eco-cool ambiance may take a bit of getting used to for the uninitiated, but the menu will convince almost anyone that meat-free cooking can be exciting and tasty. Billed "Extranational Veganism," Les Vivres's cuisine is devoid of animal products and avoids refined flour and sugar.

At lunchtime, a three-course meal costs $8.75; the price rises to $11 in the evening. It's worth it for the soup alone—especially if it's a tangy concoction mischievously called Red China. Main courses span the globe: an Indian mixed curry plate, Asian stir-fries, Middle Eastern dips and spreads. Desserts, like truffles and ice cream, are excellent, despite the lack of dairy.

Les Vivres is also known for its mega-sandwiches. The Viet is made of ginger, tofu, daikon, mint, and coriander; the Végé Lox is filled with carrot, seaweed, capers, and creamed tofu; the BLT innovatively replaces bacon with smoked coconut. On weekends, a full-out vegetarian breakfast is $7.25, including coffee or chai.

Hours: Tues.–Fri. noon–midnight; Sat. and Sun.
11 a.m.–midnight
Alcohol: No
Credit cards: No
Wheelchair access: No

4434 St-Dominique (@ Mont-Royal)
(514) 842-3479
Metro: Mont-Royal

EATING
meat and potatoes

La Binerie Mont-Royal

A Québécois comfort food institution.

You'll find lots of homey fare at this old-school Québécois diner in the heart of the Plateau. La Binerie is a real relic of yester-year—the business has been passed down through an extended family over a period of 60 years. There are only a few seats in its miniscule interior, and the counter is the best place to listen to the chitchat.

A three-course meal goes for about $6.95. It starts with a thick pea soup that's almost a meal in itself. For a taste of a pure laine staple, opt for the tourtière, a savoury meat pie that's served with or without gravy (it's better with). The pâté de saumon drizzled with white sauce and the chicken potpie are a little lighter on the stomach. La Binerie also makes a tasty shepherd's pie of ground beef, corn, and mashed potato. Ask the owner to tell you the story of how the dish earned the name "pâté chinois" in French. Roast pork sandwiches and stewed beef with veg-etables round out the meaty menu.

For dessert, choose between coconut pie or a caramel-infused pudding chômeur, which literally means "unemployed pudding." Finally, there's spruce beer, a soft drink that you must try at least once in your lifetime. Made with spruce tree gum, it tastes like Pinesol—in a good way.

Hours: Mon.–Fri. 6 a.m.–8 p.m.; Sat. and Sun. 7:30 a.m.–3 p.m.
Alcohol: No
Credit cards: No
Wheelchair access: No
Vegetarian friendly: No

---

367 Mont-Royal (@ St-Denis)
(514) 285-9078
Metro: Mont-Royal

Dic Ann's

Hamburgers that go straight to your heart.

This Montreal North mainstay has been serving a particular style of hamburger for the last 40 years—a hamburger so different from the usual fast-food fare that it's worth making a trip to this kitschy roadside diner just to try it.

Chances are, after one visit you'll develop a craving for these cholesterol-laden hamburgers ($1.65), cheeseburgers ($2), or Hi Boys ($2, with lettuce and tomato). The burgers are so flat they look like they've been run over by a Mack truck: thin patties, thin buns, thin slices of cheese, and a thin sauce with bits of meat in it. You'll want at least two burgers, but order one at a time to decrease the sogginess factor. The secret here, as any regular will tell you, is in the sauce—not the sauce brune we all know and love, but a spicier, zestier version. The fries are thin, crisp, and served in a little carton ($1.40).

The paper menu features a detailed timeline of hamburger history, but you won't make it past 1885 before your order is slapped down in front of you. Dic Ann's itself appears twice on the timeline: it opened in 1954, and it set the world's record for hamburgers served in an hour (1,512) in 1997. Wow!

Hours: Mon.–Thurs.11:30 a.m.–8 p.m.; Sat. and Sun. 11:30 a.m.–10 p.m.
Alcohol: No
Credit cards: Yes
Wheelchair access: No
Vegetarian friendly: No

10910 Pie-IX (@ Charleroi), Montreal North
No phone
Metro: Pie-IX, 36 bus

Le Manoir

Beef and beer in perfect harmony.

In a landscape of suburban mini-malls, it's hard to miss Le Manoir's wood-and-stone A-frame structure. Inside, the peaked ceiling rises above a beer-hall ambiance in which appropriately meaty meals are served. The menu bears the declaration, "Our only objective is to offer high-quality food at incredibly low prices," and that's just what they do here. It's got to be one of the only places where you can actually order fèves au lard as an appetizer.

For an amazing $9.45, the Canadian Plate spotlights a number of local dishes: a large slice of savoury tourtière, a couple of giant meatballs, a tender pig's knuckle, and a baked potato. All of it is swimming in a salty gravy so brown it's almost black. The same tasty sauce coats the huge hot beef sandwich ($7.95), which is sprinkled with peas. Another vaunted topping here is the peppercorn sauce, which you can order at a small extra charge with various roast beef dishes.

Le Manoir also serves all sorts of sausage plates, with or without sauerkraut, for around $6, including knackwurst, Hungarian, spicy Italian, and chicken and herb links. The evening table d'hôte is a steal. Full meals, ranging from $10 to $15, include pasta, seafood, and chicken dishes, and, of course, steak.

Hours: 11 a.m.–11:30 p.m. daily
Alcohol: Yes
Credit cards: Yes
Wheelchair access: Yes
Vegetarian friendly: Yes

600 St-Jean, Pointe-Claire (@ Hymus)
(514) 695-2071
Metro: Lionel-Groulx, 22 and 202 bus

Montreal Pool Room

*Something steamé and
something seamy.*

Sometimes the question isn't "Where's the beef?"—it's "Where's the best hotdog in town?" Naturally, the issue is hotly contested, but any place that's been dishing up dogs since 1912 must be doing something right. The Montreal Pool Room is situated in what has long been, and to some extent still is, the city's Tenderloin district, a sketchy stretch of St-Laurent near Ste-Catherine.

The menu, if you can call it that, is straightforward. Hotdogs cost 93 cents, and they come one way: steamé. Toasté (grilled) is too modern for these guys. Order an all-dressed and you'll get a piping-hot wiener slathered in coleslaw, onions, mustard, and relish. Add your own ketchup after you've grabbed a stool at the battered metal counter. An order of patate frite is $1.30, or $1.50 for a large. The fries are huge—wide and long—and they have a soft texture, almost like mashed potato; there's vinegar aplenty to douse them with. Put it all together in the Trio ($3.99), which is made up of two hotdogs, an order of fries, and a drink.

You can't play pool here anymore, but the eating area at the rear looks a bit like a giant billiard table. It's a great place to slum it up, especially for those who like to observe human nature.

Hours: 24/7
Alcohol: No
Credit cards: No
Wheelchair access: No
Vegetarian friendly: No

1200 St-Laurent (@ René-Lévesque)
(514) 396-0460
Metro: St-Laurent

La Paryse

High-quality burgers for carnivores and herbivores.

For more than 20 years, stylish La Paryse has been satisfying the urge for a really good burger. Just a few steps from St-Denis, it feels like a house and a diner at the same time, with two small rooms that get crowded at key times.

The menu is short, but why beat around the bush? The patties here are 100 percent beef; the buns and the fixings are fresh beyond reproach. The simplest option is the Regular ($4.95), which comes with Mozzarella, tomatoes, mushrooms, pickles, onions, lettuce, mayo, and hot mustard. The Special ($5.75) takes you one step closer to total indulgence with the addition of cream cheese and bacon. Burgers are served solo; add fries or a nice side salad for about $2.

Vegetarians are not just an afterthought here. Daily soups are clearly labeled as meat-free. The real draw, though, is the trio of veggie burgers ($5.25 apiece), each more intriguing than the next. The tofu burger is served with a miso-tahini sauce, the pinto bean burger is topped with herbed sour cream, and the third option, a patty made with nuts, is adorned with cream cheese or blue cheese, apple, and mushrooms. Save room for the delectable milkshakes in vanilla, chocolate, or coffee flavours ($3.75).

Hours: Mon. 11 a.m.–10:30 p.m.;
Tues.–Fri. 11 a.m.–11 p.m.; Sat. noon–10:30 p.m.;
Sun. noon–9 p.m.
Alcohol: Yes
Credit cards: Yes
Wheelchair access: No
Vegetarian friendly: Yes

302 Ontario (@ Sanguinet)
(514) 842-2040
Metro: Berri-UQAM

Patati Patata

The hippest hamburgers on the Plateau.

Patati Patata is proof that size doesn't matter. This rocking burger joint is hugely popular, but it's so tiny that it can only accommodate a handful of diners at once. The high-topped tables are often crammed with customers gawking through the corner windows at the action on the Main.

After perusing the limited menu, place your order by filling out the form provided, customizing your toppings and condiments (there's a small surcharge for bacon and cheese). Then hand it to one of the friendly cooks behind the counter. Patati Patata's delicious, nongreasy hamburgers are round, like meatballs, and they cost only $1.50, or $4.50 with fries and salad. Other options in a bun include the Mediterranean burger, with Feta and mint; the tofu burger; and the delicate fish burger made with sole. Don't miss the Patatine ($4), a creative take on poutine—onions, peppers, and mushrooms are thrown into the usual fries-cheese-gravy mix. Try it in a nid de frites, a crunchy nest of fried onions and potatoes.

Patati Patata also offers club sandwiches, fish and chips, and a menu du jour (about $6) with a soup of the day. Freshly pressed juices, microbrews, and—for dessert—brownies round out the experience.

Hours: Mon.–Fri. 9 a.m.–11 p.m.;
Sat. and Sun. 11 a.m.–11 p.m.
Alcohol: Yes
Credit cards: No
Wheelchair access: Yes, but tables are too high
Vegetarian friendly: Yes

4177 St-Laurent (@ Rachel)
(514) 844-0216
Metro: St-Laurent, 55 bus

Taverne Magnan

Manly meals in a blue-collar bar.

Established in 1932 as a luncheonette for workers at a nearby factory, Magnan is more classic than classy. Women have only been allowed to eat in the tavern since 1989, and today's customers include gladhanding politicians, visiting actors, and sports celebrities.

With a menu that pretty much defines meat-and-potatoes dining, this place keeps the blue-collar feeding frenzy alive. The house specialty is roast beef, which Magnan boasts is as good as you get at home—lucky you, if that's the case. It's tender, the browned exterior is studded with peppercorns, and it's served au jus—and plenty of it. The price depends on the thickness of the cut. The smallest is 6 ounces, at $12.95, and the largest is an unimaginable 20 ounces. Your order comes with boiled vegetables and your choice of potato: fries, mashed, or baked.

Daily specials are usually a good deal. The featured fish ($9.45) might be a huge portion of trout, grilled and served with a herb sauce on the side. Also look out for the various Magnan festivals—the tavern claims to have started the food festival trend in this city. There's the Magnan Bierfest (sausages, sauerkraut, and strudels) in March, a mussel fest in January, and a scallop fest in July. Whatever the time of year, sample the homemade pies ($2.95), especially the delicious pecan, which is smooth and creamy like toffee.

Hours: Mon.–Fri. 6:30 a.m.–11 p.m.;
Sat. and Sun. 8 a.m.–11 p.m.
Alcohol: Yes
Credit cards: Yes
Wheelchair access: Yes
Vegetarian friendly: No

2602 St-Patrick (@ Charlevoix)
(514) 935-9647
Metro: Charlevoix

strictly EATING sandwiches

Café l'Étranger

Made-to-order sandwich mania.

Café l'Étranger's below-street-level windows offer secret views of passersby in the downtown core. Launched in 1998, this resto was designed as a place where students and shoppers could go to relax and reenergize, just far enough from the madding crowd.

The enormous array of made-to-order sandwiches—there are more than 50 to choose from—contains almost every ingredient ever to grace a piece of bread. At first glance, it seems like you'll need a PhD in food sciences just to decipher the menu. On closer inspection, you'll notice that there's a certain amount of repetition: a number of intriguing combinations are available as wraps, panini, or burgers ($7 to $9). The Bob Marley consists of jerk chicken, portobello mushrooms, corn, grilled peppers, and grilled eggplant, while the Monterey combines Monterey Jack, Cheddar, avocado, sour cream, and mushrooms. The nongreasy grilled cheese sandwiches—like the Marlon, with zucchini and red peppers—are served on lightly browned bread with a ridged texture. Plates come with salad and oddly addictive pasta chips.

Less daunting decisions await among the bargain-priced daily specials from all over the map, including New Orleans, Italy, Thailand, and California. Brunches ($6.95 to $9.95) feature fun foods like baked blueberry and candied pecan French toast, while later in the day the college crowd can choose cocktails with names like Pokémon Sucks, Survivor Shot, and Forgetaboutit.

Hours: Mon.–Fri. 9 a.m.–11 p.m.;
Sat. and Sun. 11 a.m.–midnight
Alcohol: Yes
Credit cards: Mastercard, Visa
Wheelchair access: No
Vegetarian friendly: Yes

---

680 Ste-Catherine W. (@ University)
(514) 392-9016
Metro: McGill

Café Santropol

Quirky, quaint, and quintessentially Plateau.

If one place in the city could be considered uniquely Montreal, it's the Santropol. Eccentric, relaxed, and rootsy, it's the embodiment of the Plateau's Bohemian lifestyle. The interior is charming, with its pressed-tin ceilings and mismatched mugs; the meandering layout leads to a garden that's one of the most atmospheric in the city—it has the ambiance of a French Quarter courtyard in New Orleans.

The café was opened in the mid-seventies in a successful effort to stop the demolition of a block of old buildings next to the Hôtel Dieu Hospital. The activist angle is still alive and well three decades later: the business emphasizes fair-trade foods and donates one percent of its profits to charitable community organizations like Santropol Roulant, which has students deliver meals to seniors.

In addition to healthy daily soups ($3.25), the inventive sandwiches ($6.75 to $8.25 for a triple-decker) are made with exceptional bread from a nearby Portuguese bakery. The Duluth Avenue is filled with a mixture of Brie, blue cheese, nuts, and spices; the Hazel Brown combines cottage and cream cheeses, hazelnuts, and chocolate (strawberries are optional); and the ham sandwich is layered with mint, apples, and cucumbers. The marvellous milkshakes, tantalizing tisanes, and sumptuous carrot cake are not to be missed.

Hours: Mon.–Thurs. 11:30 a.m.–12:30 a.m.;
Fri. 11:30 a.m.–1 a.m.; Sat. noon–1:00 a.m.;
Sun. noon–midnight
Alcohol: No
Credit cards: No; Interac accepted
Wheelchair access: Through rear terrace
Vegetarian friendly: Yes

3990 St-Urbain (@ Duluth)
(514) 842-3110
Metro: St-Laurent, 55 bus

Chez José

Simple snacks with Spanish spirit.

They can't fit more than 15 people at a time into this snackbar, but not for lack of trying! Chez José is often filled to capacity, and the resulting ambiance is fun-loving but fairly frantic. Its winning combination of fresh juices, sandwiches, and empanadas makes it a popular Plateau hangout at breakfast and lunch.

The food here will keep you healthy and happy. Most items sell for less than $5. Empanadas get the gourmet treatment, with stuffings that are more French than South American, such as a divine chicken divan, or a broccoli and blue cheese mixture. Sandwiches are made on the spot, and they include the Churrasco, with chicken, avocado, tomato, and cheese; and the Rockabilly, with chorizo, a Portuguese sausage. For those who shun meat, there's a veggie pâté sandwich. For brunch, Chez José whips up a wicked Spanish omelette. The crêpes are also delicious: on the sweet side, there's a decadent lemon-chocolate number; on the salty tip, there's the classic ham and melted cheese.

Last but not least, this place offers healthy shakes ($3 to $4). The Vampire is made with orange, strawberry, raspberry, and grenadine; the Pacific Dream blends orange, banana, and mango; and the Yuniko combines pineapple and strawberry.

Hours: Mon.–Fri. 7 a.m.–8 p.m.; Sat. 8 a.m.–8 p.m.; Sun. 9 a.m.–8 p.m.
Alcohol: No
Credit cards: No
Wheelchair access: No
Vegetarian friendly: Yes

173 Duluth E. (@ Henri-Julien)
(514) 845-0693
Metro: Sherbrooke or Mont-Royal

Herb's

West Coast health food on the West Island.

A favourite St-Anne's retreat, Herb's bills itself as a "little food factory"—this small-scale operation churns out vegetarian fare with a personal touch. The vibe calls to mind the early days of the California health food movement, and while the location is not exactly West Coast, the sun-dappled garden (complete with bike rack) does overlook the water.

Sandwiches ($5.30 to $6.65, tax included) are built on a foundation of whole-grain bread and served with the salad of the day. There's a tomato sandwich with spinach; avocado with red onions, Cheddar, and honey-Dijon sauce; and antipasto with cream cheese, artichokes, black olives, sun-dried tomatoes, and alfalfa sprouts. Tuna, roast beef, and ham and cheese round out the options.

The exquisite Japanese Salad ($6.45) of somen noodles, shredded carrot, and green onions is tossed with a tangy ginger-sesame dressing. The Bagel Melt ($7.95) is made with cream cheese, red peppers, avocado, maple mustard, and melted Gouda, and it's served with two different salads. There are also burritos ($7.80)—two tortillas wrapped around a bean mash, salsa, and cheese. Desserts—like banana bread and blueberry pie—are homemade, as are the fruit juices—like the sweet 'n' sour lemonade. Sunday brunch, served until 11:30 a.m., is a treat.

Hours: Tues.–Fri. 11 a.m.–7 p.m.; Sat. 11 a.m.–5 p.m.; Sun. 9 a.m.–5 p.m.
Alcohol: No
Credit cards: No
Wheelchair access: One small step
Vegetarian friendly: Yes

142 Ste-Anne, Ste-Anne-de-Bellevue (@ du Collège)
(514) 457-1150
Metro: Lionel-Groulx, 211 bus

Olive et Gourmando

Gourmet baked goods for gourmands.

Masterful baking and topnotch ingredients form the backbone of this charming Old Montreal lunch spot. Freshly prepared breads, croissants, and pastries are stacked on wooden shelves that surround a handful of tables. The scene is illuminated by large windows.

Sandwiches ($7 to $8) can be had hot or cold, but they always come on wonderful grilled bread and with a good dose of imagination. The warm apple and Cheddar combo is made with locally produced cheese, along with thinly sliced fruit sprinkled with citrus and fresh herbs. The sharp cheese plays off the sweetness of the apple to mouthwatering effect. The Cuban consists of smoked ham, braised pork shoulder, Gruyère, homemade relish, and mayo enhanced with a touch of spicy chipotle pepper. Cold sandwiches include marinated portobello mushrooms with maple mayo; and grilled, grain-fed chicken combined with guacamole, hot peppers, and mango. For an interesting variation on the ubiquitous bagel with lox, try the Gourmando version, which employs smoked trout, herbed cream cheese, capers, sun-dried tomatoes, and fresh spinach leaves.

There are several salads to choose from each day, as well as a daily soup. The sweet confections are hard to ignore—if you're lucky, the flaky pastries may still be warm from the oven!

Hours: Tues.–Sat. 8 a.m.–6 p.m.
Alcohol: No
Credit cards: No; Interac accepted
Wheelchair access: One step
Vegetarian friendly: Yes

351 St-Paul W. (@ St-Pierre)
(514) 350-1083
Metro: Square-Victoria

St-Viateur Bagel

Bagel bonanza.

A few years ago, one of the brains behind the St-Viateur Bagel shop realized that fans of these doughy rolls shouldn't always have to go home to eat them. The first bagel café was launched in the Plateau in 1996, followed a few years later by a second location in N.D.G. Both outlets have the requisite wood-burning oven and offer products to eat in or take out.

For a light snack, try a toasted bagel with a flavoured cream cheese, a Middle Eastern dip, or a spread made of tofu or smoked salmon. There are about a dozen bagel sandwiches (starting at $4.95) on the menu. The Mexi melds Cheddar, avocado, tortilla crumbs, red pepper, lettuce, and salsa; the Omerta is meaty with Italian salami, mortadella, capicollo, and Provolone; and the Wow mixes chèvre, sun-dried tomatoes, marinated eggplant, and pesto. There is also a breakfast bagel with eggs and ham and a club made with turkey instead of chicken. Of course, you can always get a bagel served the traditional way, with smoked salmon, cream cheese, onion, and capers ($8.50).

The rest of the menu lists premade salads, cakes, and specialty coffees from all over the world, as well as coffee-based drinks made with liqueurs and aromatic essences, like hazelnut, raspberry, chocolate, or vanilla.

Hours: 6:30 a.m.–11 p.m. daily
Alcohol: Yes
Credit cards: No; Interac accepted
Wheelchair access: Yes
Vegetarian friendly: Yes

1127 Mont-Royal E.
(@ de la Roche)
(514) 528-6361
Metro: Mont-Royal

5629 Monkland
(@ Marcil)
(514) 487-8051
Metro: Villa-Maria

Titanic

Funky, French, and fresh.

This luncheonette is sunk below street level—just like the ship that bears its name. It does a brisk takeout and delivery trade, but if you're a first-timer you should definitely eat onsite. In these cramped and vaguely chaotic quarters, you'll be served by the friendly, funky wait staff.

Titanic offers stunning sandwiches on a choice of breathtakingly fresh baguettes, fougasse (a herbed bread similar to Italian focaccia), or the more delicate and lightly crusty pouliche. These creations range from $4.50 to $7.50 (half-orders are available). Take your pick of combos like blue cheese and cucumber, roast pork and chutney, goat cheese and olive pesto, meatloaf and HP sauce, smoked salmon and roasted peppers, or Bocconcini and sun-dried tomatoes. The fantastic BLT on a baguette is spread with cream cheese and filled with crispy bacon, lettuce, and sliced tomato. Other sandwich ingredients will make you wish that your home larder could be so well stocked: peppery pâté de campagne, marinated chicken breast, P.E.I. mackerel, Italian sausage, and cold cuts like smoked ham, spicy Calabrese sausage, capicollo, and roast beef.

The Antipasto Misto ($9) is a great alternative to a lunch salad. The mélange of marinated vegetables changes daily—peppers, eggplant, and asparagus roasted, grilled, or marinated to perfection—and it's served with lettuce and bread. For the same price, there's always a quiche and a special of the day.

Hours: Mon.–Fri. 7 a.m.–4:30 p.m.
Alcohol: No
Credit cards: No
Wheelchair access: Through terrace
Vegetarian friendly: Yes

---

445 St-Pierre (@ St-Sacrement)
(514) 849-0894
Metro: Square-Victoria

EATING
far east feast

Chez Gatsé

Tibetan treats from the roof of the world.

Montreal's first Tibetan restaurant dispenses high-altitude cuisine at rock-bottom prices. This cozy downstairs space in the Quartier Latin has brick walls hung with colourful fabric and an oasis of greenery out back.

The soups here make great starters ($2.25). A hearty lentil concoction called tinchougna is delicious, but the chouru soup is more intriguing—and recommended only for fans of blue cheese. Momos are another Tibetan staple worth sampling. These stuffed pockets are comparable to Chinese dumplings, but their texture is distinctive. The freshly steamed dough pockets are available with beef, chicken, vegetable, or sweet cheese fillings. They're brought to the table piping hot, along with a tomato dipping sauce. Make a meal of them, or get a side order.

Main course options include Shapta ($7.85), a beef and onion stir-fry with a light gravy that has hints of Asian seasonings. The boneless Lhassa Chicken ($7.35), marinated and simmered to tenderness, is served in a delicately spiced sauce. As an accompaniment, choose between rice or tinmo, a steamed bread. Heat things up with some choko khatsé, a tongue-searing potato dish. Tibetan food is meat-centric, but vegetarians have a couple noodle dishes and soups to choose from here. Desserts are unremarkable, but the butter tea *is* remarkable—definitely an acquired taste.

Hours: Mon.–Fri. 11:30 a.m.–2:30 p.m.;
5:30 p.m.–10:30 p.m. daily
Alcohol: Yes
Credit cards: Yes
Wheelchair access: No
Vegetarian friendly: Limited

317 Ontario E. (@ Sanguinet)
(514) 985-2494
Metro: Berri-UQAM

Épicerie Kei-Phat

Surreal meals at a Pan-Asian supermarket.

Épicerie Kei-Phat is all about food. Whether you come to shop in its supermarket section or dine in the restaurant area, this establishment—at one time an IGA store—will offer you a cornucopia of Asian treats.

Perusing the menu is like looking through a family album. There are almost no descriptions of the countless Chinese, Thai, and Vietnamese dishes, just photos (some of which are hilariously blurry). To start, the wonton soup ($2.95 to $6.95) is excellent— you may want the bigger bowl. Given the setting, freshness is pretty much guaranteed, especially when it comes to fish and seafood. The Ginger Shrimp ($8.95) are lightly coated in batter, deep-fried, and served with slices of onion and ginger on a bed of lettuce. The Thai-Style Chicken ($6.95) is made with basil, three kinds of pepper, onion, a hint of hot chili, and steamed rice. Vietnamese pho soups rank among the more popular selections, but there are also barbecued duck, pad Thai, fried rice . . . if you've seen it on a restaurant menu, you can probably find it here.

After eating, you can search the grocery aisles for all the esoteric ingredients and cooking implements you'll need to re-create an exotic meal at home—bamboo steamers, dried watercress, marinated lemons, jackfruit, salted duck eggs . . .

Hours: 9 a.m.–9 p.m. daily
Alcohol: No
Credit cards: No
Wheelchair access: Yes
Vegetarian friendly: No

4215 Jarry E. (@ Pie–IX)
(514) 376-5749
Metro: Pie–IX, 139 bus

Higuma

Sit-down sushi at fast-food prices.

A newcomer to the St-Denis strip, Higuma occupies the middle ground between the fast-food sushi shop and the more formal Japanese restaurant. It's a cute, casual place with angular wooden tables inside and a tiny patio out front. And it presents its inexpensive Japanese fare with care and flair.

Everything is made to order, but this isn't a place for sushi purists. Maki, rather than sashimi or nigiri, are highlighted here, and customers are invited to choose from a list of fun, nontraditional rolls. There's the Hawaii, with pineapple, ham, and cream cheese; the Aloha, with tangerine and crab stick; and the Calgary, with deep-fried chicken, teriyaki sauce, and flying-fish roe. The less outré Spicy Salmon (five pieces for $5.50) and Spicy Tuna (five pieces for $5.75) rolls are both very tasty. Sushi combos, which include a pleasantly musky miso soup or a sesame-infused salad, are a good way to go; they start at $9.50 for 10 pieces.

Higuma also has fishless options for vegetarians, including several hosomaki of pickled radish, sweet potato, Chinese mushrooms, or cucumber (three pieces for $2.50); inari, made with sweet fried tofu ($2.50); and more complex rolls made with oshinko (pickled cabbage) and kampyo (squash).

Other Japanese dishes on the menu are worth exploring, including a delightfully crunchy tempura ($7.95); tonkatsu ($9.50), a pork chop fried to crispness and served on rice; and a grilled eel called unadon ($8.50).

Hours: noon–3 p.m. daily, 5:30 p.m.–10:30 p.m. daily
Alcohol: Yes
Credit cards: Yes
Wheelchair access: No
Vegetarian friendly: Yes

3807 St-Denis (@ Roy)
(514) 842-1686
Metro: Sherbrooke

Hong Kong Restaurant

Hong Kong–style barbecues and hot pots.

The specialty at this Chinatown mainstay is Hong Kong–style barbecued pork, duck, and chicken, but the menu doesn't stop there. It contains more than 200 items; still more are noted on pieces of paper taped to the walls.

The hot and sour soup is very good, but look beyond other Western favourites to the dishes aimed at the Chinese clientele— after all, who was General Tao anyway? The hot pots ($8.95), in particular, offer great value and refined flavours. The fish hot pot is a simmered casserole of battered white fish, soft tofu with a chewy, golden exterior, bamboo, water chestnuts, broccoli, bok choi, and Chinese mushrooms. Other hot pots combine chicken with bamboo, beef with ginger and shallots, and stuffed tofu with veggies. In winter, cook-at-your-table fondues, known as fire pots, are also available.

Other authentic offerings include chicken with lotus root, beef with bitter melon, sautéed watercress, and congee, a rice-based porridge. Hong Kong, which displays lobster and fish in tanks, also serves a lot of seafood. Peking duck is available too ($14.50 for half, $27 for a whole). This labour-intensive recipe involves rubbing the bird with seasonings, air-drying it, and then roasting it so the skin takes on that distinctive glazed look, sealing in the yumminess.

Hours: 11 a.m.–midnight daily
Alcohol: Yes
Credit cards: Yes
Wheelchair access: No
Vegetarian friendly: Yes

1023 St-Laurent (@ de la Gauchetière)
(514) 861-0251
Metro: Place-d'Armes

La Maison Kam Fung

Delicious, dizzying dim sum.

Destination: dim sum! Between 7 a.m. and 2:30 p.m. every day, there's no menu at Kam Fung—everything operates on a pick-and-point basis. Waitresses circle with carts, peddling their wares, sometimes getting stuck in traffic jams between tables. Dim sum dishes range from $3.50 to $5.50, and they are designed to be shared. Some come in bamboo steamers, others in heated metal containers. Servers let you peek inside and then they ask, "What do you like?"

Sip on the complimentary jasmine tea as you debate the relative merits of Chinese broccoli with hoisin sauce, spareribs, chicken feet, duck feet, stir-fried baby squid, or noodles with peppers. There are also many dumplings, familiar and foreign. Shrimp pot-stickers are enveloped in glutinous white pasta and have a faint taste of ginger. The mushroom dumplings consist of firmly packed shrimp and pork balls topped with a Chinese mushroom. Deep-fried half-moons are filled with a pork and green onion mixture and served in a slightly sweet pink sauce. Portions of sticky rice come wrapped in a banana leaf, studded with pork, and infused with a flavouring reminiscent of green tea. Watch for the gelatin-based desserts that jiggle on the lower shelves of the carts.

Hours: dim sum 7 a.m.–2:30 p.m. daily,
dinner 5:30 p.m.–9:30 p.m. daily
Alcohol: Yes
Credit cards: Yes
Wheelchair access: Yes
Vegetarian friendly: No

1111 St-Urbain, mezzanine (@ de la Gauchetière)
(514) 878-2888
Metro: Place-d'Armes

O-Bentò

Cheap sushi and Japanese lunch in a box.

This little restaurant is named for the Japanese lunchbox, and that's the specialty here at noon hour. Similar to an airplane meal in presentation, a bento lunch (about $8) comes in a square container divided into compartments that might contain deep-fried chicken, beef teriyaki, or shrimp and veggies encased in a fluffy tempura batter. Other compartments could hold a mini-salad with a dense lemon dressing, steamed carrots in a tangy sauce, rice, or a sushi roll.

Bento is only available at lunchtime, but there are lots of other affordable house dishes to try after dark: udon noodle soups, curries, and a particularly good donburi, a popular Japanese dish that consists of a bowl of rice topped with chicken and egg. This place also has some of the least expensive sushi rolls in town that are actually cut and prepared with quality in mind, and they're offered at only a dollar each. Rolls include standards as well as some original creations—like the deep-fried Pop roll and the Rap roll with onions.

O-Bentò is an exciting eatery because it constantly experiments with new ideas. Occupying a hidden downstairs space, it has bright-yellow walls, cheerful lanterns, and a friendly young staff— a welcome change for diners who frequent the city's typically hectic noodle shops.

Hours: Mon.–Fri. 11:30 a.m.–2 p.m., 4 p.m.–10 p.m.;
Sat. 5 p.m.–10 p.m.
Alcohol: Yes
Credit cards: Yes
Wheelchair access: No
Vegetarian friendly: Yes

1237 Guy (@ Ste-Catherine)
(514) 931-0388
Metro: Guy-Concordia

Quatre Saisons

Sizzling Korean barbecues to share with friends.

Korean cuisine is one of the hottest cuisines out there, figuratively and literally. Turn to the back of the Quatre Saisons menu—past the sushi, noodles, and teriyaki—to find some of the most inexpensive Korean specialties in Montreal. Many of these are best sampled in a group so that everyone can dig their chopsticks into a communal tabletop pot.

To start you off, the waitress will bring small bowls of marinated potatoes, steamed spinach, creamy coleslaw, seaweed, and, of course, the pickled cabbage called kimchi. Shared dishes to look for include bulgogi, strips of meat sizzling on an iron griddle; and shabu, steaming noodle soups with your choice of ingredients—from octopus to black goat. Korean barbecue combos of beef, chicken, pork, plus sushi maki are offered for one ($11.95) or two people ($26). Everything is cooked up in a slightly sweet glaze of soy, garlic, and sesame oil. Other meals under $10 include a satisfyingly spicy beef stew called uk gae jang with noodles, bean sprouts, and whole green onions, and a Korean specialty called bibimbap, a mixture of rice and seasoned meat, vegetables, and egg. For the adventurous, there's jellyfish, sliced raw meat, and even a Korean-style pizza. For vegetarians, there's bokum, a vegetable stir-fry.

Hours: 11 a.m.–11 p.m. daily
Alcohol: Yes
Credit cards: Visa; Interac accepted
Wheelchair access: Two steps
Vegetarian friendly: So-so

4200 St-Jacques W. (@ St-Ferdinand)
(514) 932-3309
Metro: St-Henri

south asian EATING sensations

Bahay Kubo

Bakery with Filipino flavours.

Serving a regular clientele from Montreal's growing Filipino community, this bakery/cafeteria is stylishly outfitted with bamboo accents and an ultramodern sign. The staff can't always translate menu items for the uninitiated, but if there's one thing the novice quickly learns when scanning the steam trays of hot food, it's that swine is prime in the cooking of the Philippines. The various stewed concoctions might be pork heart, pork with liver, pork with chicken, pork with noodles, or the ever-popular "pork with pork."

An express menu offers two choices with rice for $5.50. Balance the vaguely sweet flavours of the meats with a peppery noodle stir-fry, or a delicious stew containing chicken, pork, eggplant, string beans, lima beans, squash, and bitter melon (and they mean bitter). The arroz caldo—a soup of stewed chicken with rice—reflects the historical influence of the Portuguese in the Philippines. The precooked milkfish, or mackerel, is equally good cold or reheated.

For dessert, there are custard flans or the more tempting halo-halo ($3.50), made of creamed ice, coconut, and dried fruits of every kind. Also, every afternoon like clockwork, hot pandesal, or salted bread buns, come out of the ovens—just one of the many treats baked here.

Hours: Tues. and Wed. 11 a.m.–9:30 p.m.;
Thurs. 10 a.m.–10 p.m.; Fri. and Sat. 10 a.m.–11 p.m.;
Sun. 10 a.m.–10 p.m.
Alcohol: No
Credit cards: No
Wheelchair access: One step
Vegetarian friendly: No

4735 Van Horne (@ Victoria)
(514) 733-1841
Metro: Plamondon

Ban Lao Thai

Salads, sausage, and spicy Laotian specialties.

This modest eatery takes you to Laos, a narrow South Asian country sandwiched between Thailand and Vietnam. The menu dips into the familiar repertoire of Laos's neighbouring nations and lists a handful of harder-to-find national specialties.

Laotian dishes ($7) include chilled salads made with papaya, chicken, beef, squid, or pork. Morsels of grilled meat are tossed together with fresh cilantro, mint, bean sprouts, hot peppers, cucumber, and string beans, delighting the palate with crunchy textures and cleansing flavours. If you don't want a suicidally spicy meal, ask for medium. Other regional specialties include Laotian sausage with perfumed sticky rice, beef jerky, and deep-fried tilapia.

The rest of the menu overlaps with Thai and Vietnamese fare. To start, there are satays with peanut sauce, or the more unusual fish cakes ($3) with lemongrass dipping sauce. Main courses are under $10, including stir-fries and sautéed noodles with fresh basil, garlic, cashews, sweet and sour sauce, and red or yellow curry. Meal-size Tonkinoise soups range from $4.50 to $6.50 a bowl. Lunch plates are a deal at $4.50, and they include two miniscule shrimp-stuffed egg rolls. There are four lunch choices, including one vegetarian; offerings could include a veggie and tofu stir-fry, ginger chicken, egg noodles with beef, or pork with bamboo shoots.

Hours: Mon.–Wed. 11 a.m.–8 p.m.;
Thurs.–Sat. 11 a.m.–9 p.m.
Alcohol: No
Credit cards: No
Wheelchair access: Yes
Vegetarian friendly: Yes

---

930 Décarie (@ Decelles)
(514) 747-4805
Metro: Côte-Vertu

Cuisine Bangkok

Thai food that defies the food court.

It may be situated in a food court, but Cuisine Bangkok has some of the best Thai fare in the city. Head up to the third floor of the Faubourg shopping mall and look for the longest lineup—you'll find the owner and his wife hard at work behind the counter. Any dish that features Chinese eggplant—a narrower variety, light mauve in colour—is worth trying, as it's nearly impossible to cook it at home the way they do here. Sliced on the diagonal and fried to tenderness without a sour note, it can be had with chicken, beef, or on its own with red peppers and fresh basil ($5). Bangkok also puts out a good pad Thai, tossing noodles, seasonings, and veggies with tofu, beef, squid, or, best of all, seafood ($5.50 to $6.95). Dishes, like these, that contain peanuts are clearly labelled.

There are always meal specials here for $6.15, served with a lemongrass-infused chicken soup or two small egg rolls stuffed with vermicelli. Set plates include chicken with green or yellow curry, beef with red curry or ginger, and chicken with cashew nuts. The barbecued duck is slightly more expensive. There's quite a variety of meatless items on the list, including noodle dishes, tofu dishes, vegetable curries, and satays.

Hours: 10 a.m.–9 p.m. daily
Alcohol: No
Credit cards: No
Wheelchair access: Yes
Vegetarian friendly: Yes

1616 Ste-Catherine W. (in the Faubourg Ste-Catherine)
(514) 935-2178
Metro: Guy-Concordia

Nonya

A funky Indonesian find on the lower Main.

Nonya is an exciting Asian restaurant for budget diners because it brings together the best of all worlds: authentic eats, low prices, and style. Despite its affordability and its location on an ill-reputed block of St-Laurent, it's got the funky décor and the nouveau presentation you'd expect to find on a more upscale section of the Main. Best of all, it offers Indonesian food made with care—subtly spiced skewered meats, seafood, and rice perfumed with tamarind, coconut milk, anise, chilies, garlic, and ginger.

Most appetizers are under $3, such as the krokets of mashed potato, ground beef, and carrots; and the lumpia goreng—deep-fried rolls stuffed with finely chopped shrimp and bamboo shoots. It's worth springing for udang mangga ($5.50), four perfectly cooked shrimp arranged around a citrusy mango salsa. Main courses include gado-gado, veggies in a wonderfully subtle and textured peanut sauce; melt-in-your-mouth lamb skewers; and nasi goreng ($8), shrimps nestled beneath gently seasoned rice, topped with a fried egg and skewers of marinated beef, and served with a big shrimp cracker.

Instead of dessert, try susu soda gembira. This drink is basically do-it-yourself cream soda, except way creamier. Into the glass goes condensed milk, a thick, fuschia-coloured syrup, club soda, and ice cubes. Mix it up and experience the taste of childhood in Jakarta.

Hours: Tues.–Sun. noon–3 p.m., 6 p.m.–10 p.m.
Alcohol: No
Credit cards: Yes
Wheelchair access: One small step
Vegetarian friendly: Limited

1228 St-Laurent (@ Ste-Catherine)
(514) 875-9998
Metro: St-Laurent

Phayathai

Ultra-refined Thai.

Phayathai is a classy but casual establishment nestled in a down-town Victorian home. It's hard to go wrong here, because every-thing is delicious. The prices aren't bargain-basement, but the place does offer exceptional value at the top end of budget dining.

Soup to start is an absolute must ($3.50 to $4.50). The bowls are small but packed with ingredients. The chicken soup with coconut milk and galangal is chock-full of tender pieces of meat, button mushrooms, and spices subdued by the creamy texture. The fiery Phayathai broth is brimming with all sorts of seafood—like crab, shrimp, fish, squid, and scallops.

Main courses ($7.50 and up) are just as fascinating to the taste buds. Sliced barbecued duck ($10.50), with its crispy caramel-ized skin intact, is heavenly served in a thick, rich red sauce. The beef with basil ($9.50) comes with sprigs of fresh herbs and slivered vegetables, and it's perfectly cooked so that each bite melts in your mouth. Tofu, deep-fried fish, satay vegetables, and several shrimp dishes complete the selections.

To end your meal, there's tapioca pudding, a tropical fruit called rambutan, or pleasantly nonsugary green tea ice cream. A pot of Thai tea with a distinctive orange colour and a smoky tamarind flavour leaves a nice taste in your mouth.

Hours: Mon. 5:30 p.m.–10:30 p.m.; Tues. and Wed. noon–2:30 p.m., 5:30 p.m.–10:30 p.m.; Thurs. and Fri. 5:30 p.m.–11 p.m.; Sat. and Sun. 5:30 p.m.–11 p.m.
Alcohol: Yes
Credit cards: Yes
Wheelchair access: No
Vegetarian friendly: Yes

1235 Guy (@ Ste-Catherine)
(514) 933-9949
Metro: Guy-Concordia

Pho Pasteur

Flavourful pho, grills, and coffee from Vietnam.

If it's hot, steamy soup that you're after, Pho Pasteur gives a good bang for your buck. This family-run resto, which has been specializing in Tonkinoise temptations for 15 years, is located in a part of town that has gradually become Petit Vietnam. When you eat here you'll feel like you're sitting in someone's apartment where, though the paint may be faded, the food is fresh, fresh, fresh.

There are 20 different kinds of soup in three sizes ($4.75 to $6.95). To a base of lightly perfumed broth flavoured with hints of garlic, ginger, chili, sprigs of basil, and noodles, you can add paper-thin slices of rare steak, beef flank, tripe, barbecued pork, chicken, or seafood. The result will give you a perma-grin. Also on the menu: grilled meats with rice, vermicelli, and salad, including a pork and beef combo that's caramelized to semisweet perfection. A whole meal—with soup, imperial rolls, and grilled meat—is only $9.50.

Vietnamese coffees are another draw here. For a real kick in the pants, end your meal with a divine café filtre au lait glacé ($2.50). Some assembly is required, but the unctuous result is worth it. If you need help putting together the filtered coffee, condensed milk, and ice cubes, your server will be happy to help.

Hours: Mon., Wed., and Sun. 10 a.m.–9 p.m.;
Thurs.–Sat. 10 a.m.–10 p.m.
Alcohol: No
Credit cards: No
Wheelchair access: No
Vegetarian friendly: No

7087 St-Denis (@ Jean-Talon)
(514) 272-1341
Metro: Jean-Talon

Pho Viet

Veritable Vietnamese in a cheerful Gay Village bistro.

Take a peek at all the kitschy items in the retro boutiques on Amherst as you make your way to this cheerful restaurant. A Gay Village favourite, its orange-hued walls and framed photographs boost the ambiance a few notches from the bland minimalism of many pho soup shops. Sweet service by the owners helps too.

Meal specials are $7.50 at lunch and about $12 in the evening, tax included, for soup, salad, main, and tea or coffee. For a couple of bucks more, upgrade to a Tonkinoise soup—it's a worthy investment. Also available in a meal-sized bowl, the pho here are excellent, particularly the beef, in a complex, almost musky broth with green onions and noodles. There are many more Vietnamese specialties to try here—like grilled brochettes, ginger or curry chicken, and an Imperial sizzling platter with seafood and noodles. In the evening, the fondue for two ($21.50) is offered; simmer your own chicken, shrimp, veggies, and lemon leaves over a gas burner. Another recent addition to the menu is caramelized salmon ($10.25).

Also try the homemade Viet-style lemonade—it's like a party in your mouth. And don't overlook the desserts either, such as the fried bananas, the litchi sorbet, and a crème caramel that would put any haughty French chef to shame.

Hours: Mon.–Fri. 11 a.m.–3 p.m., 5 p.m.–9 p.m.;
Sat. 5p.m.–9 p.m.
Alcohol: BYOB
Credit cards: No
Wheelchair access: One step
Vegetarian friendly: No

1663 Amherst (@ Ontario)
(514) 522-4116
Metro: Berri-UQAM

the french **EATING** connection

Aux Derniers Humains

Eccentric, eclectic corner café.

Aux Derniers Humains is an eclectic neighbourhood café that successfully blends the café concept with full-meal service. It manages to appeal to a broad spectrum of customers while retaining a distinctively artsy ambiance.

In addition to breakfasts worth waking up for, there's the evening table d'hôte, which is much more daring and creative than you might expect from your typical corner restaurant. It's a good value at around $13 (tax included, with soup and coffee, tea, or tisane). The soup might be a surprisingly delicious banana and coconut blend in a tomato-laden broth. Daily dishes could be a risotto, a salad of chicken liver mousse with berries, or a puff pastry filled with goat cheese, sun-dried tomatoes, and caramelized onions. The regular menu lists excellent crêpes; large, multi-layered salads; and individual pizzas. Leave room for the succulent desserts, especially the stacked apple pie, which is extra-good heated up.

This is also a place to relax over coffee or to meet friends for an after-work beer. Check out a bizarre brew called Quelque Chose; it's steeped in fresh cherries, with cassis and chocolate tones— and served warm. You can also get a taste of it in the duck confit.

Hours: Tues.–Fri. 10 a.m.–11 p.m.; Sat. and Sun. 9:30 a.m.–11 p.m.
Alcohol: Yes
Credit cards: No
Wheelchair access: Two steps, but bathrooms aren't accessible
Vegetarian friendly: Yes

6950 St-Denis (@ Bélanger)
(514) 272-8521
Metro: Beaubien or Jean-Talon

La Boîte à Lunch

Picnic fixings to stay or go.

Amid the grand Victorian homes and enormous trees of rue St-Hubert, the miniscule La Boîte à Lunch is barely noticeable. This quaint neighbourhood kitchen comes complete with checkered tablecloths and a chef in a double-breasted white uniform. You can order any menu item to go, but you may want to take a seat and linger at one of the five sunny tables.

As its name suggests, La Boîte à Lunch will pack you a lunch for a long day at the office or, better yet, a picnic in nearby Parc Lafontaine. For $7.25, you get to choose from several of their fresh salads: chef, Caesar, or Greek. Next, pick a sandwich. The ham and cheese is a cut above the ordinary; the niçoise is made with tuna, hard-boiled eggs, red onions, black olives, and lettuce. A beverage is included.

Daily specials go for around $8, including soup and drink. These may include a Waldorf salad, braised pork with ginger, or a mixed plate featuring some of the chef's fancies, like a three-layer vegetable mousse, marinated eggplant, and smoked salmon. Another option is a plate of grilled vegetables, such as heart of palm, eggplant, zucchini, and tomatoes. La Boîte stops short of haute cuisine, but it's a cute alternative for fast food with Euro flair.

Hours: Mon.–Sat. 7 a.m.–11 p.m.; Sun. 8 a.m.–10 p.m.
Alcohol: No
Credit cards: No
Wheelchair access: Through terrace
Vegetarian friendly: Yes

4165 St-Hubert (@ Rachel)
(514) 527-2207
Metro: Mont-Royal

Café Souvenir

Outremont ambiance at other-side-of-the-mountain prices.

Cheap eats in the heart of Outremont—who'd have thunk it? This café serves full meals that hover around the $10 mark on a strip populated by chichi restaurants, so there's a good reason it's often packed. The ambiance is classic French bistro with a funky twist. In warm months, its cane chairs and marble-topped tables spill out onto the sidewalk, while the interior remains dark and cozy. Solo diners will feel comfortable at the curved wooden bar that overlooks a digital slide show projected onto the wall.

The menu features all sorts of Mediterranean favourites, from a simple starter of marinated Feta and olives ($2.95) to classic steak-frites ($10.95). Other fare includes burritos, quesadillas, and a couscous merguez ($8.95) in a light tomato-based sauce brimming with vegetables. Sandwiches ($4.95, or $7.50 with fries or salad) include BLTs, veggie burgers, and merguez or Toulouse sausage on a baguette. Daily specials are a good deal at $12, including an appetizer and a cup of Souvenir's excellent coffee. Look out for the Caesar salad with grilled fish instead of chicken.

This place caters to all tastes at just about any time of day. It's also popular for its all-day breakfast that features omelettes, waffles, and pain perdu, along with healthier options, like yogurt with fruit and freshly squeezed juices.

Hours: Sun.–Thurs. 7 a.m.–11 p.m.; Fri. and Sat. 7 a.m.–midnight
Alcohol: Yes
Credit cards: Yes
Wheelchair access: One step
Vegetarian friendly: Yes

1261 Bernard W. (@ Champagneur)
(514) 948-5259
Metro: Outremont

Finzi

Mediterranean meals in Old Montreal.

Opened in early 2003, this undiscovered bistro serves up Mediterranean fare along with a few French classics. The high-ceilinged Old Montreal location is outfitted with banquettes, bright tablecloths, and waiters in semiformal dress. It's much more popular at lunchtime than after working hours, which simply means there's more room for the rest of us in the evenings.

The menu here offers a much higher-end experience than you can normally find for the price. It begins with your choice of several different appetizers, all $3.95: soup of the day or minestrone, Caesar salad or Bocconcini and tomatoes. Other hunger-management essentials, like artichokes, olives, and marinated salads, are laid out on a buffet table for your salivating pleasure. The 20 or so main courses are priced at $9.50 across the board. On the list you'll find mussels prepared any way you like, confit de canard, steak-frites, warm liver salad, and salmon tartare. In addition, there's always a fish of the day. Finzi also specializes in Italian fare, such as linguine with shrimp, stuffed cannelloni, eggplant Parmigiana, and veal osso bucco—plus you can get a taste of well-prepared pasta on the side of many dishes.

For desserts like crème caramel or chocolate mousse, add $1.50 to your bill. For a glass of wine, add $5.50.

Hours: Mon.–Fri. 11 a.m.–2:30 p.m.; Thurs.–Sat. 4 p.m.–10 p.m.
Alcohol: Yes
Credit cards: Yes
Wheelchair access: Yes
Vegetarian friendly: Limited

20 Notre-Dame E. (@ St-Jean-Baptiste)
(514) 398-0942
Metro: Place-d'Armes

Le Grand Comptoir

Classic French bistro fare.

It's not easy to find real French food prepared by real French chefs at really un-French prices, but Le Grand Comptoir manages to offer classic dishes that won't set you back too many francs. Although it's been decorated on a shoestring, the place somehow feels like a genuine Parisian eatery—maybe it's the aroma of Continental cooking that lends an air of authenticity to the room.

Menu items are listed on chalkboards, with lots of choices around the $15 mark, soup included. The bavette aux echalottes is excellent—a thin steak cooked up with green onions and served with fabulous fries and salad with a creamy dressing. Thicker cuts of meat, like the entrecôte, are available with several different sauces. Other choices include Toulouse sausage, salade niçoise, and Atlantic salmon drizzled with Chablis sauce ($11.95). You'll have to fork over a little more for the duck confit, the steak with Roquefort sauce, or the cassoulet, a slow-cooked casserole of white beans and various meats.

Those unfamiliar with the French penchant for animal innards should ask the helpful waiters for explanations before ordering rognons, ris de veau, or a tripe sausage called andouillette. But whatever you choose, consume it French-style—with at least a demi-carafe of red wine.

Hours: Mon.–Wed. 11:30 a.m.–9 p.m.; Thurs. and Fri. 10:30 a.m.–10 p.m.; Sat. noon–9 p.m.
Alcohol: Yes
Credit cards: Yes
Wheelchair access: Through terrace
Vegetarian friendly: Barely

1225 Philips Square (@ Ste-Catherine)
(514) 393-3295
Metro: McGill

La Petite Marche

Charming Mediterranean café with crowd-pleasing dishes.

La Petite Marche is a real crowd-pleaser. It brings together a menu of Mediterranean faves at reasonable prices at a thoroughly unpretentious St-Denis location. You'll find it just a couple of blocks north of the major shopping strip, and it's a welcoming place to unwind on a weekday afternoon.

The table d'hôte goes for $10.95 (with soup, dessert, and coffee or tea). Make your selection from among six French and Italian specialties, one of which is bound to tickle your fancy. First, soothe your hungry tummy with a homey soup of the day, which might be a super-savoury, fortifying concoction of tomatoes, onions, and chickpeas. A typical lineup of main dishes includes Swiss salad, with mixed greens, ham, cheese, fresh fruit, and veggies; a chicken breast in a sumptuous sauce; or manicotti. Pastas are big here—cheese tortellini with green onions, mushrooms, Parmesan, and orange zest; or shells with bacon, capers, and shallots.

The regular menu includes yummy creations like lamb with fresh basil sauce ($12.95), a picture-perfect coquille St-Jacques, and fresh fish filets such as trout or salmon. The crêpes are also excellent, especially those done al forno, a process that seems to enhance their creamy richness. With its consistent charm, La Petite Marche hops at breakfast too.

Hours: 8 a.m.–11 p.m. daily
Alcohol: Yes
Credit cards: Visa; Interac accepted
Wheelchair access: No
Vegetarian friendly: Yes

5035 St-Denis (@ Laurier)
(514) 842-1994
Metro: Laurier

Le Triskell

Crêpe crazy.

Crêpes bretonne supposedly originated in Brittany, in northern France. These paper-thin pancakes, cooked on a large circular griddle, are commonly made of buckwheat flour, which has long been produced in the region. Cozy, rustic Le Triskell adheres to tradition in preparing its crêpes, offering about 20 variations on the theme, both sweet and savoury.

A plain crêpe starts at $3.25, and the price rises as fillings are added. A classic combo of egg, sausage, and mushroom is $9.50. Alternately, you can mix and match your ingredients, choosing standards like ham, cheese, seafood, béchamel, and asparagus. The $12.50 table d'hôte gets you soup or salad, a dessert—like crème caramel or apple pie—a drink, and a crêpe with a combination of any three fillings or a seafood filling. Other prix-fixe choices include omelettes, chef's salad, or filet of sole. You can also order appetizers à la carte, such as broccoli au gratin, garlic snails, onion soup, or heart of palm salad.

Another possibility here is a dessert-only outing. Le Triskell dishes up delightful crêpes filled with chestnut cream ($6.50), lemon, banana, almond paste, peach, pear, and, of course, chocolate. But, for the record, it's definitely not too decadent to eat one crêpe for a main course and another for dessert!

Hours: Mon.–Thurs. 11:30 a.m.–11 p.m.;
Fri. 11:30–midnight; Sat. noon–midnight;
Sun. noon–11 p.m.
Alcohol: Yes
Credit cards: Yes
Wheelchair access: Yes
Vegetarian friendly: Yes

3470 St-Denis (@ Carré St-Louis)
(514) 281-1012
Metro: Sherbrooke

EATING
old-world cooking

La Caverne

Slavic specialties in an underground Russian resto.

If you've been searching for affordability and authenticity in a Russian restaurant, La Caverne is for you. The sign outside might suggest that it's a 2-for-1 pizza joint, but inside you'll find lovingly made Slavic food and a jovial atmosphere—complete with music and dancing on weekends.

Among the appetizers are five kinds of soup, from borscht to solana. Also look out for the refreshing marinated Asian carrots ($2.99), one of several dishes with Siberian and Mongolian influences. The mysteriously labelled "herring under coat" is an exquisite, layered square of beet salad, shredded carrot, and mild fish ($3.50).

The house dish is pogrebok ($11.99). It consists of three potato patties coated in a crunchy breading and stuffed with ground beef, mushrooms, and a herbed egg mixture. This specialty comes with pickles, and tomato sauce and sour cream for dipping. Dumplings are another specialty here, from pelmeni filled with ground beef and coriander to lamb-stuffed Asian-style manty with mild red sauce. Don't miss La Caverne's incredible sour cottage cheese vareneki ($4.99 to $6.99), which also come stuffed with cherries, potato, mushrooms, or cabbage. Be sure to check out other regional dishes, like dolma (vine leaves stuffed with mint and meat), troika (eggplant, green pepper, and tomatoes with meat), blini made of thin crêpes, doughy deep-fried tcheburek, and homemade pot roast—all guaranteed to be the real thing and ranging in price from $1.75 to $10.

Hours: 10 a.m.–10 p.m. daily
Alcohol: BYOB
Credit cards: Yes
Wheelchair access: No
Vegetarian friendly: Yes

5184 Côte-des-Neiges (@ Swail)
(514) 738-6555
Metro: Côte-des-Neiges

Chez Better

European sausage specialists.

The menu at Chez Better mines Europe east and west for sausages and brings them all together in a casual bierhaus atmosphere. On the list: wiesswurst from Bavaria, curried links from Holland, Toulouse and boudin blanc ("white pudding") from France, Viennoise from Austria, and debreziner from Hungary— just to name a few. Sausages are served with plump brown fries and mouthwatering sauerkraut. On the low-fat tip, check out leaner wieners made with chicken, veal, ostrich, or bison, which come with salad for added healthiness.

For maximum variety, tasting platters are the way to go. On the Swiss Plate ($10.95), you'll find a mild schublig sausage along with crisply breaded chicken schnitzel, fries, salad, and the house mayo. For a real lesson in contrast, try the trio of white bratwurst; smoky-spicy, flavour-packed cevapcici from the Balkans; and the almost-too-hot-to-handle Italian diable ($9.95). Another meal option here is steamed mussels with all sorts of sauces, from Pernod to rosée to dijonnaise ($11.95 to $14.95). Consider also sharing a Swiss fondue to start ($8.95).

The sausage selections here are outnumbered only by the international beers. Chez Better emphasizes German and Belgian brews, and there's a house brand on tap.

Hours: Noon–9 p.m. daily; open later in summer
Alcohol: Yes
Credit cards: Yes
Wheelchair access: One small step
Vegetarian friendly: No

---

160 Notre-Dame
(@ St-Vincent)
(514) 861-2617
Metro: Champ-de-Mars

5400 Côte-des-Neiges
(@ Lacombe)
(514) 344-3971
Metro: Côte-des-Neiges

EuroDeli Batory

A little corner of Poland.

EuroDeli Batory specializes in Polish fare: imported groceries, pastries, and homemade meals. On weekends, it's packed with ex-pats who pop in after services held at the church next door. They swarm the aisles and take over the few tables at the front. There's been talk of expansion, which would allow everyone a little more breathing room.

The food here is ridiculously cheap. The borscht ($2), overflowing with veggies in a beet broth, has an added zing that's guaranteed to clear out your nasal passages. The pierogi ($4)—mushroom, cheese, or meat—are exquisitely fresh and have a distinctive home-cooked feel. A mixed platter, only $12.50, features cabbage rolls, pierogi, dumplings, and goulash. Another option is krokietyz miesem, rolled crêpes stuffed with shredded meat or cabbage and mushrooms, covered with a mushroom sauce, and served with salad and slaw. The bigos stew harmoniously blends kielbasa sausage and sauerkraut.

At Batory, you can also pick up wonderful packaged soups and cookies, as well as a selection of cured meats and baked goods from behind the counter. The poppy seed cake, in particular, is great with coffee. Don't forget to buy a bag of frozen pierogi to cook at home.

Hours: Tues. 10 a.m.–6 p.m.; Wed. 10 a.m.–7 p.m.; Thurs. and Fri. 10 a.m.–9 p.m.; Sat. 10 a.m.–4 p.m.; Sun. 9 a.m.–2 p.m.
Alcohol: No
Credit cards: No; Interac accepted
Wheelchair access: No
Vegetarian friendly: Limited

115 St-Viateur (@ St-Urbain)
(514) 948-2161
Metro: St-Laurent, 55 bus

Le Georgia

Authentic fare from former Soviet republics.

The closest thing this ultra-authentic eatery has to décor is the parade of food photos in the window featuring dishes from Russia, Poland, and the republic of Georgia. Opened in the summer of 2002, this small resto is the place to sample lovingly prepared cuisine from the former Soviet Union.

There are two great soups to choose from. The more familiar borscht is an infusion of beets and other veggies, while the less-well-known ocrochka is a cold soup made of potato, egg, ham, green onion, dill, and cucumber in a refreshing, milky base ($3.50). For something else out of the ordinary, try a traditional Georgian dish called satsivi ($4.10)—chunks of chicken in a subtly spiced sauce thickened with ground walnuts. Satsivi is served chilled, and you're meant to eat it with your hands and the bread it's served with. Another specialty is a labour-intensive creation called tchanaki, a meat and vegetable stew topped with pastry dough ($7.50).

The array of homemade dishes includes veal aspic, red beans, and eggplant caviar, as well as pelmeni and vareneki (dumplings). Stuffed crêpes—with potatoes, meat, or cheese—are $2.99 with mushroom sauce and $2.50 with cream sauce, while a delicious beef Stroganoff meal is only $4.50. Afterwards, coffee is served in china cups. Premade items are also available to go, including Russian bread baked on the premises.

Hours: 6 a.m.–10 p.m. daily
Alcohol: No
Credit cards: No
Wheelchair access: One step
Vegetarian friendly: Limited

5112 Décarie (@ Queen Mary)
(514) 482-1881
Metro: Snowdon

Mazurka

Old-style Polish dining room.

One of the granddaddies of Montreal's ethnic eating scene, this Polish restaurant exudes a certain jaded charm. It's been a fixture on Prince-Arthur since the 1960s, when the street was a hotbed of hippie culture. The strip is still a magnet for those seeking impromptu street entertainment and inexpensive meals, and Mazurka's prices have remained among the lowest on the block.

The price tag for the popular meal specials varies according to a complex formula that depends on time of day and day of the week, but the top price is $5.95. That includes coffee and a choice of soup (opt for the borscht or pea rather than the chicken noodle). The main-course list covers all the standards: meat pierogi or cheese and potato pierogi with fried onion; blintzes with sweetened cottage cheese; potato pancakes; or bigos, a delicious pork-cabbage-sausage stew. Mixed plates, offered at the same low price, include a good combination of meat and vegetarian entries. There's usually a special of the day, as well— often an omelette. For more substantial eating, go à la carte. Expect to pay around $12 for standbys like chicken Kiev, schnitzel, and pig's knuckles.

If you're in the mood for adventure, Mazurka won't blow you away, but if you want the comfort of age-old favourites, it's waiting there for you.

Hours: Noon–11 p.m. daily
Alcohol: Yes
Credit cards: Yes
Wheelchair access: Through terrace
Vegetarian friendly: Limited

---

64 Prince-Arthur E. (@ Coloniale)
(514) 844-3539
Metro: Sherbrooke or St-Laurent

Schwartz's Montreal Hebrew Delicatessen

Smoked meat central.

Schwartz's storefront is hung with a selection of cured meats that are the health food equivalent of politically incorrect. Inside, there's no elbowroom, it's loud and it's chaotic, but this is where you'll have the true Montreal smoked meat experience—the one that tourists and locals alike find so irresistible. This legendary little deli opened on the Plateau in 1930, when the neighbourhood was home to many of the city's Jewish immigrants.

The Schwartz philosophy seems to be, "Smoke it, and they will come." Each day, beef briskets are marinated and cured on the premises, without preservatives, resulting in a rich, peppery flavour and a distinctive pink colour. A classic order is a medium smoked meat sandwich on rye ($4.25), with mustard, a half-sour pickle, and an order of fries (lean, as they say, is for sissies). A cherry cola is a strangely effective digestive aid.

Although they're often overlooked, other house specialties are worth trying. The smoked chicken, available as a combo for $11.95, is studded with peppercorns and falling off the bone. Schwartz's will also grill up a mean steak, fry up some liver, or make sandwiches of stuffed chicken, kosher salami, tongue, or turkey. Smoked turkeys are available during the holiday season.

Hours: Mon.–Thurs. 9 a.m.–12:30 a.m.;
Fri. 9 a.m.–1:30 a.m.; Sat. 9 a.m.–2.30 a.m.;
Sun. 9 a.m.–12:30 a.m.
Alcohol: No
Credit cards: No
Wheelchair access: Yes
Vegetarian friendly: No

3895 St-Laurent (@ St-Cuthbert)
(514) 842-4813
Metro: St-Laurent, 55 bus

Wilensky's Light Lunch

Sandwiches for the shtetl.

Entering Wilensky's is like stepping back in time. Little has changed at this 70-year-old lunch counter since author Mordecai Richler hung out here as a child. It's an enduring landmark from the era when Mile End (where Richler set *The Apprenticeship of Duddy Kravitz*) was the heart of Montreal's vibrant Jewish community. Wilensky's walls are lined with old newspaper clippings, and seating is limited to a few wobbly bar stools from which you can watch the staff interact.

Besides hotdogs and chopped-egg sandwiches, there's pretty much one thing to order here: a mystery-meat concoction called the Special. Actually, it's made with bologna, and it goes for $2.50 ($2.90 with Kraft cheese, $3.10 with Swiss). Specials are created on a sandwich press that looks like it dates back to the Industrial Revolution. Most customers get more than one, accompanied by a dill pickle or a half-sour (80 cents).

For most of us, used to canned cola, a hand-pumped soda ($1.05) is a kick. It's fun to watch these fizzy drinks being mixed—they contain sugar, carbonated water, and a flavoured syrup, like cherry, chocolate, pineapple, or root beer. Milkshakes are $1.85. Dessert comes in the form of candy bars, toffee, or Cracker Jack.

Hours: Mon.–Fri. 9 a.m.–4 p.m.
Alcohol: No
Credit cards: No
Wheelchair access: No
Vegetarian friendly: No

34 Fairmount W. (@ Clark)
(514) 271-0247
Metro: St-Laurent, 55 bus/Laurier, 51 bus

EATING
mideast treats

Al-Taib

Fresh, fast, and frenzied Arabic bakery.

Although it's basically a fast-food restaurant, Al-Taib is a cut above the average late-night shawarma stand in terms of freshness and variety. It also seems to be trying to set a record for speedy service: the moment you enter, you can hear the servers shouting, "Next! Next!" while darting back and forth between the ovens and the counter.

An absolute must-try here is zaatar, a disc of dense pita bread spread with oil and a magic mixture of herbs and spices. It's rolled up with crispy turnip, sprigs of fresh mint, onions, tomatoes, shredded lettuce, and olives. The zaatar, with its lingering flavour of thyme, is a refreshing sandwich, and it only costs a loonie—$1.50 with cheese.

Al-Taib also specializes in baked goods, which are displayed inside a glass counter. With most items hovering around $2, you can't go wrong if you just pick and point at random. The fatayer, tasty triangles filled with spinach or cheese, are delicious. So is the lahmajine, an Arabic pita pizza topped with ground meat, tomatoes, and onions, and liberally sprinkled with herbs. Traditional thick-crust pizza is surprisingly good here too—try a slice with the chicken topping for a taste that's hard to find elsewhere. There's also a salad bar featuring tabouleh, chickpea, and bean salads, priced by weight.

Hours: 24/7
Alcohol: No
Credit cards: No
Wheelchair access: No
Vegetarian friendly: Yes

2305 Guy (@ de Maisonneuve)
(514) 931-1999
Metro: Guy-Concordia

Au Vieil Istanbul

Low-key Turkish delights at lunch.

Turkish food is hard to define, but it all becomes clearer when you remember that Constantinople, now Istanbul, was once the hub of the world's trade routes. And conquerors from the mighty Ottoman Empire picked up a few culinary tips when they invaded parts of North Africa and Europe.

This mingling of influences makes Au Vieil Istanbul an intriguing destination, especially at lunchtime, when rustic, kasbah cooking is showcased. There are always two noon-hour specials, ranging from $7.49 to $9.99. It might be Albanian spinach, stuffed eggplant, or a Turkish version of moussaka. Featured dishes change daily, but the lineup for the week is listed on the menu, so you can plan a return visit for baked spinach borek, made with filo pastry, or terbiyeli kefta, sweet and sour meatballs in creamy lemon sauce.

Lunch dishes are not available in the evening, but you can still eat at this quaint and homey resto for $15. The focus shifts to Turkish-style pizzas and shish kebabs, served with excellent rice pilaf, salad, and potatoes. Two people can make a light meal out of the Meze Tabagi ($13.99), a six-appetizer platter that includes superb fried carrots in yogurt. Finish up with figs or a throat-scorching shot of a potent liquor called raki.

Hours: Mon. 11:30 a.m.–3 p.m.; Tues.–Sat. 11:30 a.m.–10 p.m.
Alcohol: Yes
Credit cards: Yes
Wheelchair access: No
Vegetarian friendly: Yes

1247 Bleury (@ Ste-Catherine)
(514) 864-6095
Metro: Place-des-Arts

Chase

Refined Lebanese fare at restrained prices.

Chase is a casual neighbourhood restaurant with a dual-level terrace overlooking busy Monkland in the heart of N.D.G. Inside, the décor is just nice enough for a sit-down supper outing, and the place is often filled with locals lapping up the Lebanese fare.

To taste a lot for as little expense as possible, opt for one of three mixed Oriental platters ($8.95), which highlight elements from the long list of appetizers. That means dips like hummus or baba gannouj; salads like tabouleh or fattouche; pastries filled with cheese, spinach, or meat; falafel balls with tahini; and stuffed vine leaves. The vegetarian combos are just as varied ($7.95 to $8.45), with additional choices like eggplant-based moussaka and moudardara made with lentils, rice, and onions.

Chase is a real deal at lunch, when $6.50 specials allow for savings on regular menu prices, and pita sandwiches are $3.45. At dinner, generous main courses are a decent value at $9 and up for grilled meats, fish, and seafood. Don't let the complimentary dish of pickled veggies distract you from worthy appetizers like spicy makanek sausages, or kebbeh neyeh, the Middle Eastern equivalent of steak tartare. A dinner for two, including a medley of brochettes (shish taouk, ground beef kefta, and shish kebab), hummus, baba gannouj, fattouche salad, and rice can be had for $25.

Hours: Mon.–Sat. 11 a.m.–10 p.m.; Sun. 11 a.m.–9 p.m.
Alcohol: Yes
Credit cards: Yes
Wheelchair access: No
Vegetarian friendly: Yes

5672 Monkland (@ Harvard)
(514) 482-2256
Metro: Villa-Maria

Chez Benny
Fast food, Israeli-style.

Is this Montreal or Tel-Aviv? It's loud, it's crowded, and everyone's pushing their way to the cash to make their orders heard. And somehow, despite the din, the Benny's staff always seems to get the orders right. This no-frills eatery provides fast food for the kosher crowd in the form of a quick Middle Eastern fix.

Be warned: Benny's may change the way you think about falafel. Moist, dense, and fluffy, these deep-fried ground chickpea balls are practically falling apart. Their texture is much looser than that of the variety many of us are used to. Like most of the dishes, the falafel can be ordered as a sandwich ($4) or as a plate ($7.50, with three choices of salad). The all-dressed sandwich is the way to go, stuffed into three-quarters of a thick pita pocket, spilling over with sauce and vegetables. It's a mess to eat, but it's worth getting your hands dirty!

Almost as good are the kefta meatballs on a baguette and the mixed-salad plate ($6 to $8), featuring a variety of dips and marinated legumes. From the fridge, help yourself to one of the imported nectars—they're not as thick as they look, and they come in flavours like mango, peach, and pear.

Hours: Sun.–Thurs. 10 a.m.–11 p.m.; Sat. 4 p.m.–11 p.m.
Alcohol: No
Credit cards: No
Wheelchair access: Yes
Vegetarian friendly: Yes

5071 Queen Mary (@ Snowdon)
(514) 735-1836
Metro: Snowdon

Khyber Pass

Aromatic Afghan cuisine in a cozy setting.

The cuisine of Afghanistan has hints of the cooking of neighbouring countries—Iran, Pakistan, Tibet, and even China. But it really spotlights the grilled meats and simmered stews that are suited to its rugged landscape and nomadic past. Khyber Pass, Montreal's only Afghan eatery, is cozy and thoughtfully decorated, a reminder of the good aspects of a nation too often in the news.

To start, there's a dense, chapati-like bread to dip into three sauces—peppery yogurt, refreshing green coriander, and tangy red pepper. If you're having just one appetizer, overlook the yummy steamed dumplings and go for the even yummier Bonami Citrouille ($4.95): slices of fried pumpkin doused in an unusual sauce that tastes of cardamom, ginger, and chilies. It's Halloween and spice tea rolled into one!

Kebabs and simmered meats dominate the main courses. Lamb brochettes are served with basmati rice in three different colours. The slow-cooked chicken kabuli palaw is smothered in rice sprinkled with raisins and shredded carrot. Although the cuisine is meat-oriented, vegetarians will find a mixed platter containing spinach, eggplant, gumbo, cauliflower, and much more, "cooked the Afghan way," for $11.95. The four-course table d'hôte is a good value, but to eat for under $15 you'll have to go à la carte—then share a cardamom-flavoured pudding for dessert.

Hours: 5 p.m.–11 p.m. daily
Alcohol: BYOB
Credit cards: Yes
Wheelchair access: Three steps
Vegetarian friendly: Yes

506 Duluth E. (@ Berri)
(514) 844-7131
Metro: Mont-Royal

Le Petit Alep

Sumptuous Syrian fare in a busy bistro.

This funky Syrian and Armenian bistro is the baby sister of the more upscale Alep restaurant next door. The food is less expensive here, but it's prepared by the same skilled cooks.

For a starter to knock your socks off, try the sweet and spicy mouhamara dip, a lumpy mash of breadcrumbs, pomegranate molasses, cayenne, and ground walnuts ($2.25). A mazza appetizer ($3.25) includes slices of cucumber, tomato, toasted pita, and mild Alep cheese. Dunk these elements in olive oil and then dip them into a bowl of zaatar to dust them with spices and herbs, such as thyme and sumac.

The flexible menu caters to people in search of a full meal or just a snack. For a quick fix, there are several sandwiches, like spinach sabanegh, and salads, like the delightfully lemony fattouche. Marinated meats are served on pita or as a light meal accompanied by a seasoned rice and noodle mix, and a fresh, crispy salad. The shish taouk here is unbelievable ($5.25 or $8.50)—chunks of chicken bursting with flavour and tenderness. The kebab osmally is like tahini quicksand—juicy pieces of beef brochette sinking into a sesame sauce. To end things on a sweet note, order mehalabié ($3), a rosewater and milk pudding that's light and cool on the tongue.

Hours: Mon.–Fri. 11 a.m.–11 p.m.; Sat. and Sun. 9:30 a.m.–11 p.m.
Alcohol: Yes
Credit cards: Yes
Wheelchair access: Yes
Vegetarian friendly: Yes

---

191 Jean-Talon E. (@ de Gaspé)
(514) 270-9361
Metro: Jean-Talon

Tehran

An Iranian meatfest.

The menu at this recently renovated Iranian restaurant is very straightforward: just a handful of choices printed on a single sheet of paper. All the meals include pita bread, soup or salad, a copious main course, and tea. The two combination plates are the most expensive items, at just over $15 each (tax included), but there are plenty of cheaper offerings.

The soup is often a heavy-duty concoction of spinach, lentils, beans, and noodles in a tasty lamb base, topped with a blob of yogurt in the shape of a flower. The salad is a simple mix of iceberg, cukes, and tomatoes made a little more special with a thick herbed dressing.

The house specialty is marinated meats accompanied by basmati rice fragrant with saffron. The kabab barg ($13) is a marinated filet mignon, scored with a knife for added tenderness. The zereshk polo, chicken in tomato sauce, is the stuff that cravings are made of (your choice of leg or breast, $10). A tangy flavour permeates the meat, accented by zesty barberries, a fruit similar to the red currant. Vegetarians can try mirza ghasemi ($10), a purée of eggplant and tomato infused with garlic and Persian herbs.

Despite the nonsmoking, nondrinking environment, Tehran attracts customers of all ages, and the atmosphere can get boisterous.

Hours: noon–11 p.m. daily
Alcohol: No
Credit cards: No
Wheelchair access: No
Vegetarian friendly: Limited

5065 de Maisonneuve W. (@ Claremont)
(514) 488-0400
Metro: Vendôme

Bombay Choupati

Discover Bombay and Madras in a mini-mall.

The growth of immigrant communities on the West Island has turned what was once a culinary wasteland into a good destination for authentic eats. Located in a nondescript mini-mall, Bombay Choupati offers hard-to-find dishes from Bombay, as well as distinctive cooking from the southern Madras region.

The menu presents choices for both fussy and adventurous eaters. There are many appetizers under $5, such as the fantastically spiced goat meat patties; Bombay behl, a savoury version of Rice Krispies; and Bombay papri chat, wafers garnished with potatoes, chickpeas, yogurt, and chutney.

The Madrasi Fire Dosa ($5.95), a large stuffed crêpe, crusty and red, embodies the pleasure-pain duality. Like the other dosas, steamed idlis, and lentil fritters, it's served with a thin stew called sambar. On the mild side, the butter chicken is excellent, and it's served in a delightfully thick and creamy sauce ($8.95). Butter chicken, tandoori chicken, and goat vindaloo also come as thali ($6.95 to $8.95), a meal-in-one plate that includes vegetable curry, rice, and nan. For dessert, there's kulfi, homemade ice cream with saffron and pistachios. Finish with paan, a betel leaf containing spices and herbs designed to cleanse the palate.

Hours: Tues.–Thurs. 11 a.m.–2 p.m., 5 p.m.–10 p.m.;
Fri. 11 a.m.–2 p.m., 5 p.m.–11 p.m.;
Sat. 11 a.m.–11 p.m.; Sun. 11 a.m.–10 p.m.
Alcohol: Yes
Credit cards: Yes
Wheelchair access: Yes
Vegetarian friendly: Yes

5011 des Sources, Pierrefonds (@ Gouin)
(514) 421-3130

Bombay Mahal

Indian binge on a budget.

This restaurant's loyal fans know that if they can abide the some-what erratic service, then they will be rewarded with freshly prepared dishes at incredibly low prices. The menu is a mass of $4.99s and $5.99s; they swirl before your eyes, making it hard not to over-order, so be aware that the portions are amazingly generous.

The lineup here is a good mix of regional specialties. To start, try samosas with channa (chickpeas), lentils, or homemade yogurt. There are at least a dozen vegetable-based dishes to choose from. The vegetarian thali plate, a full meal on a metal platter, comes with richly flavoured dal, rice, and two main selections, one of which could be curried potato in a sauce as thick as honey. The bindi masala, freshly chopped okra mixed with toma-toes and onions, is also excellent. Southern Indian dosas, large folded crêpes served with sambar, a soupy vegetable stew, are popular too.

The chicken tikka here isn't the usual red colour, but this tasty brochette of white meat has a divinely spiced exterior. The Tandoori Mixed Plate ($10.99) includes a chicken leg, chicken tikka, and seekh kebab made of ground lamb. Lamb, goat, and chicken are available as kormas with yogurt and almonds, as rich curries, or with saag (spinach).

Hours: Tues.–Sun. 11 a.m.–10:30 p.m.
Alcohol: No
Credit cards: No; Interac accepted
Wheelchair access: No
Vegetarian friendly: Yes

1001 Jean-Talon (@ Birnam)
(514) 273-3331
Metro: Acadie

Ganges

Heat-seeking Indian specialties in elegant surroundings.

Ganges is a cut above your average bargain-priced Indian restaurant, and it's a good choice for those occasions when you're in need of a little more décor and TLC. Brick walls, warm lighting, and tabletop heating grills add to the refined atmosphere, but the reasonable prices and copious portions offer good value.

Most importantly, this N.D.G. fave serves some harder-to-find dishes that don't hold back on the heat, all for under $10. Spice seekers will be happy to see the warnings in the menu indicating that these preparations are not for the faint of tongue. Among the searing Ganges specialties is the chicken jhal frezi ($8.80), a copious plate of tender meat simmered with fresh green chilies, garlic, and peppers. Shahi rezala, a mélange of sweet, sour, and hot flavours, consists of cubed lean beef in a tangy homemade sauce garnished with red chilies. The vindaloo beef, though more common, benefits from the kitchen's liberal use of red chilies and lemon juice.

Among the appetizers, the chottpotti is worth a sample. It's made of yellow peas, potatoes, tamarind, coriander, Spanish onion, and green chilies. The vegetable-filled samosas will melt in your mouth. There's also a vegetarian combo for two ($26.95), which includes pappadam, onion bhaji, pakura, saag paneer, aloo ghobi, pickles, raita, tandoori roti, and dessert.

Hours: Mon.–Sat. 11:30 a.m.–2 p.m.;
Mon.–Sun. 5 p.m.–10:30 p.m.
Alcohol: Yes
Credit cards: Yes
Wheelchair access: Yes
Vegetarian friendly: Yes

6083 Sherbrooke W. (@ Hingston)
(514) 488-8850
Metro: Vendôme, 105 bus

Jolee

Dosas, rotis, vada, and more Sri Lankan stuff.

Sri Lankan and South Indian food is an exciting alternative to the northern Indian fare found at many Montreal restaurants. This southern cuisine is generally less heavy, less saucy, and less expensive—the whole Jolee experience costs less than $10, and it includes the free Bollywood hits that play on the restaurant's TV.

Two kinds of deep-fried cakes called vada (75 cents each) make good appetizers. The vada masala, consisting of whole lentils, hot red chilies, onion, mustard seeds, and coriander, is like cornbread and spicy falafel combined. The other vada, made of lentil flour, is like a savoury donut. Each comes with an incredible moist and fluffy chutney made with shredded coconut, curry leaves, and chilies.

Another South Indian staple, kothu roti, is a plate of chopped pita-like bread, onion, egg, and your choice of meat (up to $6). It's all tossed together like a dry stir-fry and served with a wedge of lime. Dosas, large folded crêpes made with rice and lentil flour, can be had plain or with a variety of fillings. The dosa masala ($4.50) is stuffed with a vegetable mixture and comes with a bowl of sambar—a stew of carrots, green beans, squash, onions, eggplant, and lentils infused with a decent dose of hot stuff. Rice noodles called "string hoppers" are another specialty.

Hours: noon–11 p.m. daily
Alcohol: No
Credit cards: No
Wheelchair access: Yes
Vegetarian friendly: Yes

5495-A Victoria (@ St-Kevin)
(514) 733-6362
Metro: Côte-Ste-Catherine

Malhi Sweet

Generous portions of Punjabi fare.

When it comes to budget Indian, Malhi Sweet rates high on many people's lists. The walls are garish blue and the satellite TV blares, but the crowds don't flock here for the décor. The real draw is fresh and tasty Punjabi fare at rock-bottom prices.

Main courses, served in generous portions, go for as little as $5, and appetizers are around $2. Channa samosa makes an excellent starter. It consists of crispy samosas, roughly chopped so that the potato filling comes loose, then doused in yogurt and topped with a medley of peas, garbanzo beans, sliced onions, coriander, and hot sauce.

Malhi prepares creamy sauces with pride. Fans of butter chicken will be happy to see it priced at just $7. The chicken tikka masala has similar ingredients: boneless breast meat cooked with bell pepper, onion, ginger, garlic, cream, and spices. There are several lamb and beef dishes to make your selections from, including the spicy beef madrasi and the minced meat seekh kabab, served with nan, salad, and chutney. There's also a good selection of vegetable-based dishes, like a korma of cauliflower, broccoli, peas, beans, and tomatoes melded in a thick sauce. Note the menu's odd disclaimer: "Some ingredients not visible after cooking." No problem—it all tastes great!

Hours: Wed.–Mon. 11 a.m.–11 p.m.
Alcohol: Yes
Credit cards: No
Wheelchair access: No
Vegetarian friendly: Yes

---

880 Jarry W. (@ Wiseman)
(514) 273-0407
Metro: Jarry, 193 bus

Masala

Low-fat North Indian cooking.

Masala is probably best known as a cooking school. For a long time, it was located in a cozy Old Montreal loft. Over the years, it developed a loyal following, particularly among people who work in the area, many of whom took courses there. In 2002, Masala launched a low-key lunch spot in a storefront space, but in the evenings the establishment still welcomes those who want to learn how to cook Indian at home.

The emphasis here is on healthy, low-fat dishes based on recipes from the northern provinces of Punjab and Kashmir. The moment you enter Masala, you can smell all those wonderful spices brought to you by the letter C simmering away—things like cumin, cardamom, cayenne, chilies, cinnamon, and coriander. Meals here are determined by what the friendly chef-teacher-proprietor decides to prepare that day.

The vegetarian plate starts at $8.95. It's a good spread of rice, dal, and two meatless main dishes—usually a serving of mixed vegetables and a dish inspired by whatever fresh produce has caught the chef's eye, be it cauliflower, peas, cabbage, or eggplant. Other recurring entrées include tandoori chicken, butter chicken, and the popular house specialty chicken masala, cooked with yogurt, which could be described as "korma lite." A combo plate that brings together stewed beef with curry and chicken is $13. While Masala is actually a lunch spot, dinner for groups can be arranged.

Hours: Mon.–Fri. 11 a.m.–3 p.m.
Alcohol: No
Credit cards: No; Interac accepted
Wheelchair access: Yes
Vegetarian friendly: Yes

---

995 Wellington (@ Ann)
(514) 287-7455
Metro: Bonaventure or Square-Victoria

Shaheen

Unpretentious Indian and Pakistani fare.

The box of Kleenex on every table pretty much sums up the Shaheen experience: the place may be a short on style, but it's long on thoughtfulness. Little touches like this—along with budget-friendly prices, warm service, and fresh Indian and Pakistani fare—diminish the effect of the ultra-forgettable décor.

On the small whiteboard above the counter you'll find the daily specials listed. A full meal—including soup, main course, rice, dessert, and tea or coffee—starts at $6.25 in the evening and $4.95 at lunchtime. There are always one or two vegetarian selections on the list, such as eggplant curry, mixed vegetables, or aloo mottor made with potatoes and peas. Specials begin with a plain lentil soup, but other appetizers—like samosas, stuffed paratha breads, and chaatt ($2.99), an unusual blend of apples, potatoes, chickpeas, herbs, and raisins in yogurt—are worth trying.

The specials of the day, like kofta meatballs in a thick gravy, and the mains from the regular menu all come with soup, rice, dessert, and coffee or tea. Those options priced over $10 are more intriguing and subtly executed; they include creamy kormas, tikka murga, and aromatic stir-fries called baltis. Desserts are homemade, and many of the selections are puddings that are far less sugary than a lot of Indian sweets.

Hours: 10 a.m.–10:30 p.m. daily
Alcohol: BYOB
Credit cards: No
Wheelchair access: Two steps
Vegetarian friendly: Yes

---

758 Beaubien E. (@ Christophe-Colomb)
(514) 904-0156
Metro: Beaubien

EATING
latino flavours

El Amigo

Pupusas and other Salvadorian specialties.

In recent years, the former Italian stronghold around Marché Jean-Talon has exploded with Latin American eateries purveying authentic home-style food at modest prices. El Amigo, a casual corner diner decorated in every imaginable shade of green, dishes up heaping helpings of Salvadorian, Mexican, and Spanish favourites.

Start with pupusas, an increasingly popular Hispanic street food made of white corn flour, hand-shaped into pancakes, stuffed with pork, beans, and/or cheese, and grilled ($1.40). They're served with salsa and pickled cabbage, called curtido. Other flavourful starters are beautifully blackened plantains with sour cream, fried yucca, or chicken tamales cooked to a golden colour with a hint of jalapeño, cheese, and corn.

Carne asada (grilled beef) is the star of one very manly Salvadorian house specialty. The Plato Tipico #2 ($11.95) consists of strips of pleasantly salty beef, broth-simmered rice topped with chorizo sausage, fresh tomato and onion salsa, a salad of sliced avocado, a pool of black beans, and a chunk of mild, Feta-like cheese. Another house dish is pollo encebollado—chicken topped with a tangy tomato-onion sauce ($9.95). There are still more enticing items: seafood paella and other Spanish-style casseroles, as well as traditional Mexican dishes like tacos, burritos, and enchiladas, all under $10. Strictly non-smoking.

Hours: 11 a.m.–11 p.m. daily
Alcohol: Yes
Credit cards: Yes
Wheelchair access: Two steps
Vegetarian friendly: Limited

---

51 St-Zotique E. (@ Ste-Dominique)
(514) 278-4579
Metro: Beaubien, 18 bus

Café Brazil

Fruit, feijoada, and fun.

For inexpensive exotica, the resolutely cheerful Café Brazil is the place to go. The blender at this tiny, no-frills hole-in-the-wall is kept busy whipping up an assortment of fruit and veggie shakes ($3 to $3.75), with ingredients like pineapple, mint, banana, peanut butter, orange, mango, guava, coconut milk, and papaya.

This is also a good place to grab a quick bite. Rustic and meaty feijoada ($12), the Brazilian national dish, is made here on weekends. The centrepiece is a bowl of stewed black beans, pork on the bone, pork sausage, chunks of beef, and garlic fried to a crispy gold. It's accompanied by rice, collard greens, and farofa, a mixture of chewy fruit, onion, egg, and bits of pork cooked up with cassava.

Salads are often improvised on the spot by the owner. The potato salad ($5.50) is made with green beans, dill, and eggs, while the Café Brazil ($10) includes quail eggs, heart of palm, xuxu, mango slices, green onions, shrimp, Brazil nuts, and cashews. There are also lots of little snacks available for about $2—like chicken balls, shrimp cakes, and kebbeh. Many of these finger foods are of Arab, German, and Asian origin, in keeping with Brazil's amazing blend of ethnicities.

Hours: Mon.–Fri. 10 a.m.–8 p.m., later on weekends
Alcohol: No
Credit cards: No
Wheelchair access: One step
Vegetarian friendly: Yes

5390 du Parc (@ St-Viateur)
(514) 270-7001
Metro: Place-des-Arts or Parc, 80 bus

La Chilenita

Empanada empire with Chilean charm.

La Chilenita bills itself as "la casa de las empanadas," and its doughy South American snacks are among the best in the city. The list of fillings ranges from traditional to trendy, borrowing ingredients from all over the world. For instance, La Napoletana ($1.90) contains artichokes, green olives, tomatoes, goat cheese, and Mozzarella, while the Espagnola is reminiscent of a sausage sandwich, complete with mustard. Other treats include the deliciously blended veggie-mushroom, the simple spinach and Ricotta, and the seafood stuffing of clams, crab, and scallops in a white wine sauce tinged with coriander.

This drop-in spot also serves excellent sandwiches, which empanada aficionados tend to overlook. The Pollo Palta ($3.50) is a freshly grilled chicken breast with avocado on tasty bread. The Chacarero is filled with a thin piece of steak, tomatoes, avocado, and green beans. Vegetarians have two sandwiches to choose from, one with grilled tofu.

La Chilenita recently began offering larger meals, most centered on Mexican specialties like quesadillas, burritos, fajitas, and tacos. Check the chalkboard for featured dishes ($6), like fried fish or enchiladas suza, made with chicken in a red sauce, topped with melted cheese, plus rice and red beans.

Hours: Mon. 10:30 a.m.–5 p.m.; Tues., Wed., and Sun. 10:30 a.m.–6 p.m.; Thurs. and Fri. 10:30 a.m.–7 p.m.
Alcohol: No
Credit cards: No
Wheelchair access: No
Vegetarian friendly: Yes

4348 Clark
(@ Marie-Anne)
(514) 982-9212
Metro: St-Laurent, 55 bus

152 Napoléon
(@ de Bullion)
(514) 286-6075
Metro: Sherbrooke

Irazu

Costa Rican to the core.

Irazu is named for Costa Rica's most famous volcano, situated in the rain forest. This cozy little restaurant may be a popular Latin American hangout, but it's very gringo-friendly—even when the karaoke machine is going strong.

The food here is more homey than spicy. There's a wide variety of grilled meats, like pollo (chicken), bisteca (beef), chicarron (pork), and salchichon (sausage), as well as seafood soup and all manner of other pescado (fish) and camarones (shrimp) dishes. For an appetizer, try the ceviche, raw fish marinated in citrus; or the vigoron ($5.50), a Nicaraguan dish that mixes textures and temperatures—it's made with marinated cabbage, tender chunks of yucca, and pieces of browned pork.

Follow that up with carne casado. Casado means "married," and here a delicious steak is married to fried egg, copious amounts of rice, black beans, potatoes, salad, and wonderfully moist plantains. For about $10, it's an absolute feast; and you can get the same platter with chicken or pork. Other dishes to look for include shrimp with garlic ($12.95), fajitas, and arroz con pollo. The latter dish is so familiar in Latin culture that people joke that they might have chicken with rice one night and rice with chicken the next.

Hours: Tues.–Sun. 5 p.m.–11 p.m.
Alcohol: Yes
Credit cards: Yes
Wheelchair access: One step
Vegetarian friendly: Limited

1028 St-Zotique E. (@ Christophe-Colomb)
(514) 279-0027
Metro: Beaubien

La Selva

Peruvian surf and turf.

Behind La Selva's large corner windows is a dark-walled interior filled with wonderfully worn wooden tables of different shapes and sizes. If you're not looking for anything remotely nuevo Latino, this family-run neighbourhood place is perfect for enjoying the South American classics. And, as a bonus, you can bring your own wine.

The food here is earthy and simple—fish and meat prepared the Peruvian way. There's not much more to your plate than meets the eye. The table d'hôte ($12.50) offers good value: vegetable soup, main course, coffee, and dessert. Your server will tell you about the daily specials. These often include fish—such as tilapia, shark, or trout—that benefit from being thrown on the grill without fuss. Plates come with rice, beans, and salad. Another house specialty is pollo en salsa di mani, a boneless breast of chicken smothered in a spicy peanut sauce. The same sauce is used in the ocopade camarone, made with potato and shrimp. The so-called small steak should satisfy a big appetite, and a vegetarian plate is also available.

If you're ravenous, start with an appetizer like the fish chowder, stuffed potatoes, or the hearty but plain fish soup. Desserts such as chocolate mousse or Jello aren't exactly autentica, but they add a sweet touch to a satisfying meal.

Hours: Tues.–Sat. 5:30 p.m.–11 p.m.
Alcohol: BYOB
Credit cards: No
Wheelchair access: One step
Vegetarian friendly: Limited

---

862 Marie-Anne E. (@ St-André)
(514) 525-1798
Metro: Mont-Royal

Super-Marché Andes

Pan-Latina tienda offering mountains of food.

The mountain range for which this place is named travels the length of South America; Super-Marché Andes itself offers Montrealers a taste of the national cuisines that the range traverses—from Colombia to Argentina—with a little Mexico thrown in. The original branch on the Main is considerably smaller, while the second location, further north, is almost an empire: part travel agency, part grocery store, part butcher shop, and part cafeteria-style restaurant.

Andes is a great place to compare and contrast street snacks from different countries. If you're in search of a quick bite, choose from a wide range of tamales ($3.50 to $5), made with cornmeal steamed to firmness and filled with pork, chicken, peas, egg, and other ingredients. Or try an empanada ($1.50)—a bright-yellow Colombian version stuffed with ground beef, or the Chilean-style in a pastry crust.

At the counter, you can order Mexican-style tacos and fajitas, delicious pupusas, plantains, grilled chicken, sausages, and chicharrón—crispy fried pork skin. A tip for the food-shy: ask what's in the soup of the day and listen carefully to the answer. What sounds like "gazpacho" could be "estomac de vaco" (beef stomach). The shelves here are filled with South American staples like rice, beans, and dried whole chilies, so stock your pantry.

Hours: Mon.–Wed. 9 a.m.–6 p.m.; Thurs. and Fri. 9 a.m.–9 p.m.; Sat. 9 a.m.–5 p.m.
Alcohol: No
Credit cards: No
Wheelchair access: Yes
Vegetarian friendly: Limited

4387 St-Laurent
(@ Marie-Anne)
(514) 848-1078
Metro: St-Laurent, 55 bus/
Mont-Royal, 97 bus

436 Bélanger
(@ St-Vallier)
(514) 277-4130
Metro: Jean-Talon

Taquería Sol y Luna

All tacos, all the time.

Sol y Luna takes the taco stand to new heights, with an uplifting atmosphere, brightly painted walls, and textured tablecloths. There are about a dozen taco variations on offer at this authentic Mexican eatery, and the majority are served open-faced on soft corn and flour tortillas, with green and red salsas on the side.

Tacos are served four to a plate ($6.50 to $8). The Al Pastor is topped with marinated pork, onion, coriander, and pineapple, while the savoury Pibil is made with shredded chicken, achiote chili sauce, and red-tinged pickled onion atop a layer of black beans. Vegetarians can try Nopal cactus and melted cheese, zucchini, and corn, or a folded version stuffed with mushrooms and fried onions. For less than $2, you can order Mexican rice or refried beans as accompaniments. To start, try the tortilla soup ($3), a soothing combination of soggy and crisp; the light tomato broth is dotted with sour cream. Alternately, the guacamole makes a refreshing appetizer.

In addition to imported cerveza (beer) and wine-free sangria, there are a couple of Mexican beverages to hydrate you. Agua de horchata is a cinnamon-tinted rice water, while agua de tamarindo is like iced tea with a trace of tamarind.

Hours: Mon.–Thurs. 11:30 a.m.–9:30 p.m.;
Fri. 11:30 a.m.–10 p.m.; Sat. 12:30 p.m.–10 p.m.;
Sun. 4:30 p.m.–9 p.m.
Alcohol: Yes
Credit cards: No; Interac accepted
Wheelchair access: No
Vegetarian friendly: Yes

5701 Côte-des-Neiges (@ Côte-Ste-Catherine)
(514) 739-1616
Metro: Côte-Ste-Catherine

EATING pizza and panini

Café Electra

Panino perfection.

More than anything else, Café Electra has simplicity and fresh-ness working in its favour. Sure, the location is good—a few steps from St-Laurent, it's a quiet oasis in contrast to its neighbours on the Main. And the décor is cute: whitewashed brick walls, bistro tables, big bright windows, and a counter station where the all-in-the-famiglia cooking is done. The venue, like the menu, is charming but small: it can only handle a half-dozen customers at one time. The blackboard lists various types of panini, those crusty, crispy Italian sandwiches, along with a few pizzas. And that's about it.

Sandwiches hover around the $6 mark, and they always hit the spot. Some of the cold cuts on offer include spicy calabrese, milder mortadella, capicollo, salami, roast beef, prosciutto, and its little brother prosciuttino. Different combinations of these cold cuts find their way into the panini along with marinated veggies, making for a crispy, crunchy, refreshing lunch. Tuna and vegetarian panini are also available. For two bucks, you can add one of Electra's refreshing salads to your plate; it's well worth the investment.

The excellent pizzas will run you about $8.50 to $9. They come with toppings like tuna and olives or artichokes. It's like you made it yourself, only better.

Hours: 10 a.m.–6 p.m. daily
Alcohol: No
Credit cards: No
Wheelchair access: Two steps
Vegetarian friendly: Yes

24 Pine E. (@ St-Laurent)
(514) 288-0853
Metro: St-Laurent, 55 bus

Café Milano

A true taste of Mondo Italiano.

Café Milano is the caffeine-addled pulse of St-Leonard, Montreal's suburban Italian enclave. It started out as a small social club where men from the 'hood would meet for an espresso and a little conversation, but it's since undergone a couple of expansions. Now the place has three distinct areas behind its green-and-white striped awning: the kitchen, where simple fare is whipped up; the dining room; and a gathering place for those looking for gossip and games like fuzbol.

Place your order at the counter, and a server will bring it to your table in a plastic basket when it's ready. But first, make your selection from the list of five sandwiches ($5 to $7). The sausage sandwich tops the charts—a spicy medley of meat, marinated eggplant, grilled peppers, lettuce, and tomato. The grilled chicken and the steak are almost as good, and they're filled with the same colourful condiments. Your other choices are tuna or vegetarian. The house salad ($5.50) adds some fibre and the zing of balsamic vinegar to your meal, but it's a fairly plain assemblage of lettuce.

To drink, there's San Pellegrino, Brio, or Santal juices. You'll need a beverage to keep your throat moist as you try to talk above the din. Do not, however, leave this establishment without trying the house coffee—it's to die for.

Hours: 24/7
Alcohol: Yes
Credit cards: No
Wheelchair access: No
Vegetarian friendly: Yes

5190 Jarry E., St-Leonard (@ Lacordaire)
(514) 852-9452
Metro: Jarry, 193 bus

Euro-Deli

A quick bite on the Main.

In summer, you don't need a sign to find this Main mainstay. Just look for a crowd of people sitting outside on the stoop, watching the action of the Plateau. Euro-Deli is sort of a daytime extension of Montreal clubland.

This place serves basic Italian fare that's a cut above the ordinary, in a cafeteria format. You order at the counter, and you can see your plate being assembled. The spinach and cheese calzone ($2.95) achieves a new level of greatness when doused in tomato sauce then sprinkled with cheese and a few hot chili flakes. Other calzones (cut from a large pie) include ham and cheese, or sausage and cheese. The eggplant Parmigiana ($5.95) is good too, in a pleasantly soggy way. The rest of the menu is filled with pastas and pizzas. In the first category, look for the cheese tortellini with pesto, and the aglio e olio, made with garlic, parsley, peppers, and anchovies. The plain cheese pizza—simple but satisfying—is another good bet for a late-night repast. There's usually a salad or two to choose from as well.

Desserts include tiramisu, plump cannoli, and a cake of the day. Some of the fresh pastas and sauces are sold for home consumption.

Hours: Sun.–Wed. 8:30 a.m.–2 a.m.;
Thurs.–Sat. 8:30 a.m.–4 a.m.
Alcohol: No
Credit cards: No
Wheelchair access: No
Vegetarian friendly: Yes

3619 St-Laurent (@ Prince-Arthur)
(514) 843-7853
Metro: St-Laurent

Momesso

Satisfying subs and no-fuss grub.

Momesso is a no-fuss Italian diner in a neighbourhood that could easily be dubbed Little Little Italy. It's situated on a pleasant block containing a whole row of ristorantes. Former Canadiens hockey player Sergio Momesso is a co-owner, which explains the plethora of sports posters and snapshots of team members chowing down at the counter.

Submarine sandwiches are the big attraction here. They start at $4.75 for a 7-inch and escalate to $10 for a deluxe 14-inch affair. They're served on fresh buns with a delicate crust, and one of the most popular is the sausage sub, packed with grilled meat, lots of shredded coleslaw, onions, and tomatoes. Hot pepper chutney is optional. Other possibilities include a grilled chicken sub and a veggie version. Want a meaty sub that you can really sink your teeth into? Try the Spencer steak sub with cheese and mushrooms; or go for the Supreme, which combines both sausage and beef. Oof!

On Momesso's menu, pizzas are filed under "miscellaneous," as are burgers and fries. But don't overlook these small wonders. The pizzas are only about the size of a 45, but with their simple tomato sauce and fresh, doughy crust, they sing. About $2.25 buys you a plain; sausage goes for $5.25. As you might expect, you can order cappuccino or espresso to top off your meal.

Hours: Tues.–Sun. 7 a.m.–11:30 p.m.
Alcohol: Yes
Credit cards: No
Wheelchair access: No
Vegetarian friendly: Yes

5562 Upper Lachine (@ Old Orchard)
(514) 484-0005
Metro: Vendôme, 90 bus

Motta

Premade meals and treats.

Motta is situated plunk in the middle of one of Montreal's hottest food zones. If you don't have time to buy ingredients from Marché Jean-Talon, located around the corner, you can pick up all sorts of fabulous premade meals here. The seafood pie, chock-full of fish, scallops, and shrimp, is a creamy delight encased in a light crust, and a half-portion ($3.50) can easily serve two. Round it out with salads sold by the gram: bean, artichoke, bow-tie pasta with pesto, and grilled vegetable, to name a few. There's also slab pizza ($3 to $5) with Bocconcini, spinach, or sausage, as well as dense calzones.

Motta expanded its list a few years ago to include daily specials, which can be enjoyed in the seating area or on the covered terrace. There are usually several pasta dishes, along with some veal and chicken concoctions. Meals include ciabatta with grilled veggies and soup ($5.99), or cannelloni in a tomato sauce with salad ($6.99). The newer evening table d'hôte, served from 5 p.m. until closing, is priced at $9.95 for pastas, like gnocchi and manicotti, or $11.95 for meat dishes. The price includes vegetarian or meat antipasto.

Of course, no Italian food shop would be complete without a baked goods section, and Motta offers enough sweet treats to put anyone's nonna to shame.

Hours: Mon.–Fri. 9 a.m.–9 p.m.; Sat. and Sun. 9 a.m.–7 p.m.
Alcohol: No
Credit cards: Yes
Wheelchair access: Two steps inside and out
Vegetarian friendly: Yes

---

303 Mozart E. (@ Henri-Julien)
(514) 270-5952
Metro: Jean-Talon

Napoletana

Naples-style pizzeria in Little Italy.

There's a reason why a cliché becomes a cliché: so many people agree that it works. As far as restaurants go, Napoletana has been working a tried-and-true Italian formula for 50 years. There's the semi-rustic mural on the dining room wall, the checkered tablecloths, the good, hearty food, and the unwritten rule that dinner table discussions must be held at full volume.

The fare here is pizzas and pastas, in that order. The kitchen turns out perfectly crispy, chewy squares of thin-crust pizza in the Neapolitan style ($8.75 to $14.50). The Mediterranea, with Mozzarella, tomato sauce, blue cheese, and sun-dried tomatoes, is mouth-puckeringly tasty, while the Quattro Formaggio is a cheesy delight. Other toppings include artichokes, smoked turkey, roasted red peppers, prosciutto, and eggplant.

As for pastas, the list includes spaghetti alle vongole (with clams); fettuccine Montecarlo, with asparagus, bacon, and egg; creamy tortellini alla panna; and farfalle with blue, Parmesan, and Romano cheeses. A plate of spicy sausages alla rocco is $9.50, and there are also a few salads. Prices include taxes. Napoletana is situated in Little Italy, and its terrace overlooks Dante Park, where you can stroll off the tiramisu or watch a game of bocce ball.

Hours: Mon. and Tues. 11 a.m.–11 p.m.; Wed. and Thurs. 11 a.m.–midnight; Fri. and Sat. 11 a.m.–1 a.m.; Sun. noon–midnight
Alcohol: BYOB
Credit cards: No
Wheelchair access: Two steps
Vegetarian friendly: Yes

---

189 Dante (@ de Gaspé)
(514) 276-8226
Metro: Jean-Talon

Tasty Foods

Pizza parlour with a light touch.

The walls of Tasty Foods are dedicated to a celebration of the Décarie Expressway—they are lined with old photos of the sunken highway. The ambiance of this restaurant retains something of the 1950s too. Maybe it's the perky service, the rootbeer on tap, or the oldies soundtrack.

The food also harkens back to a time when things seemed simpler. Tasty Foods serves strictly old-school pizza—none of that newfangled thin-crust stuff. Pizzas sell for $8.45 each and are available with a regular or (in a single concession to modern tastes) whole-wheat crust. The Tasty Foods Special is a carnivorous extravaganza of bacon, smoked meat, and ground beef (but don't order it if you like a crispy crust; it's so heavily laden that it barely gets cooked through). The more restrained ground-beef pizza comes with a thick coating of tomato sauce and chunks of browned meat scattered here and there. The vegetarian pizza features sliced tomatoes, green peppers, and fresh mushrooms. Other toppings include pepperoni, pineapple, hot banana peppers, and olives.

What sets Tasty Foods apart from other pizza parlours is its light, nongreasy product. No additives or preservatives are used, and the Mozzarella is made with skim milk, reducing the fat content. While it would be hard to call it healthy, this pizza comes pretty close.

Hours: Mon.–Thurs. 11 a.m.–10 p.m.;
Fri. and Sat. 11 a.m.–11 p.m.; Sun. 4 p.m.–10 p.m.
Alcohol: Yes
Credit cards: Yes
Wheelchair access: Yes, but the bathrooms are not accessible
Vegetarian friendly: Yes

6600 Décarie (@ Vézina)
(514) 739-9333/1721
Metro: Plamondon or Namur

the italian battalion

EATING

Café International

Trad meets trendy in the heart of Little Italy.

Smack-dab in the middle of Little Italy is Café International, a favourite haunt of locals in need of coffee or food at just about any time of day. The décor may be a bit tired—it seems pretty much stuck in the late 1980s—but the terrace is a great base for people-watching.

There's a $12 table d'hôte at lunch, and affordable à la carte meals are offered at dinner. Choices run the gamut from marinated meats to tender risottos to pastas with intricate sauces—such as ziti with pesto, cream, red onions, prosciutto, artichokes, and fresh basil. Other enticing combinations include grilled sausages with rapini, roasted red peppers, and potatoes; and vermicelli allo spezzatino di vitello, with shredded veal, leeks, rapini, sun-dried tomatoes, smoked Mozzarella, and white wine.

Appetizers can be somewhat pricey, but the antipasto plate is great for sharing. It features grilled vegetables—like peppers, eggplant, and asparagus—along with three kinds of marinated mushrooms, black olives, Bocconcini, tomato, prosciutto, and mixed greens tossed with a vinaigrette. Sandwiches on ciabatta (from $7.95) are served with salad, and they can be made with such elements as smoked Provolone, roasted pancetta, buffalo Mozzarella, and goat cheese. Pizzas (from $6.95) are another good bet. The menu includes wine suggestions. In summer, frozen espresso and cappuccino will help you cool off.

Hours: Sun.–Thurs. 7 a.m.–1 a.m.; Fri. 7 a.m.–3 a.m.;
Sat. 8 a.m.–3 a.m.
Alcohol: Yes
Credit cards: Yes
Wheelchair access: One step; access also through terrace
Vegetarian friendly: Yes

6714 St-Laurent (@ St-Zotique)
(514) 495-0067
Metro: de Castelnau

Café Presto

Classic Italian eateria.

Busy Café Presto takes you to Italy by way of New York City. This downtown bistro is run by two quirky brothers: one tells waiting customers that a table will be available in two minutes (when in fact it may take a little longer); the other is the chef. The interior is adorned with 1950s celebrity shots, a *Big Night* poster, and bottles of olive oil.

The daily dishes, written on a whiteboard, go for an incredible $3.95. All the extras—appetizers, drinks, desserts—are added to that. The soup ($2.25) is usually something hearty, like a minestrone. The green salad ($1.75) is tossed with an oil and vinegar dressing. Main courses are simple and simply delicious. The chicken cacciatore is a leg stewed in tomato sauce with thick slices of mushroom, served with pasta. The diable sausage is devilishly good and wonderfully spicy. Other choices might include manicotti primadonna, stuffed with cheese and spinach; penne arrabbiata; linguine paradiso; rigatoni napoletana; or calypso salad.

You'll have time to eye the desserts while you're standing in line: Amaretto cake, tiramisu, and cannoli; all are great with an excellent cup of espresso. When you pay the bill, they ring a little cowbell signalling a "met accompli."

Hours: 11:30 a.m.–3 p.m., 4:30 p.m.–9:30 p.m. daily
Alcohol: Yes
Credit cards: No
Wheelchair access: No
Vegetarian friendly: Yes

1244 Stanley (@ Ste-Catherine)
(514) 879-5877
Metro: Peel

Elio Ristorante

Back-to-basics pasta and pizza place.

Sometimes you have to get off the main drag to find the real deal. Elio is situated on the southern periphery of Little Italy, a few blocks from the commercial sector, on an otherwise unimpressive street. Given the location, its popularity is a testament to the quality of the pasta and pizza it produces. Much of the business here is takeout, but Elio does have a terrace and several nondescript dining rooms.

The pasta is homemade—this will become obvious when you take your first bite of cavatelli, fusilli, tortellini, spaghetti, fettuccine, linguine, or rigatoni. The array of 10 sauces includes Elio's special pink sauce—a cheesy, creamy rosé. It's also the base for the gigi with pancetta, olives, and onions. Pastas range in price from $5.50 for a small to $11 for a regular, which should really be referred to as huge. The baked pastas are particularly delicious; these include cannelloni, lasagne, and ravioli.

Thin-crust and traditional pizzas are created to order with ultra-fresh toppings. These are available in five sizes, from $6.50 for a nine-inch to $19 for an extra-large, which will feed five adults.

Hours: Sun. and Mon. noon–10:30 p.m.;
Tues.–Thurs. noon–midnight; Fri. and Sat. noon–2 a.m.
Alcohol: Yes
Credit cards: Yes
Wheelchair access: Two steps
Vegetarian friendly: Yes

351 Bellechasse (@ Drolet)
(514) 276-5341
Metro: Beaubien

Pane e Vino

Trattoria that blends simplicity and style.

Bread and wine—the name of this simple yet stylish trattoria says it all. Pane e Vino offers high-end Italian cooking at low-end prices. It's only open for lunch, and the airy space is often crowded with workers from nearby buildings.

Every course has a fixed price. Appetizers—such as a robust eggplant Parmesan or an antipasto plate—are $3.95. All the main courses are $8.95, including classics like veal osso bucco, a pasta trio, and grilled Italian sausage. There's also a surprising amount of seafood to be had: marinated octopus salad, mussels marinara, grilled shrimp, and the popular salmon tartare. The fried calamari, tender squid in a light batter, comes with a tangy dipping sauce and a fresh salad of mixed greens. A fish of the day, served with rice and vegetables or salad, is always offered. For a health-conscious gourmet lunch, the warm goat cheese salad is a good bet.

Desserts are within tempting view, in a glass case near the cash. Browse through the nice selection of red and white wines, or opt for a fine cup of coffee to help you get through the rest of the afternoon. The downtown location also serves breakfast from 7 a.m. to 10 a.m.

Hours: Mon.–Fri. 11 a.m.–3 p.m.
Alcohol: Yes
Credit cards: Yes
Wheelchair access: One step
Vegetarian friendly: Yes

---

212 St-Jacques
(@ François-Xavier)
(514) 844-9991
Metro: Place-d'Armes

1080 Côte du Beaver Hall
(@ Belmont)
(514) 871-1777
Metro: Bonaventure

Pasta Tre Colori

Shop or stay for honest, homemade fare.

This grocery store–cum–restaurant has a wonderful small-town feel to it, especially when the sunlight streams in through the windows. The green-and-white tablecloths, pasta posters, and fridges full of food set the tone for a casual and comforting meal. You can check out the selection of eats on a whiteboard, or look behind the counter where the homemade pastas and sauces are displayed.

Meals range from $8.50 to $9.25. They start with slices of crusty bread and salad or a soup—such as a vegetable-laden minestrone, or stracciatella, made by whisking eggs into steaming broth. Main courses are pleasantly simple and unquestionably fresh. A typical lineup might include linguine vongole, ravioli napoletana, and spaghetti bolognese. The manicotti is stuffed with a mild cheese and spinach mixture and topped with the sauce of your choice, such as the spicy house arrabbiata. The meat-stuffed tortellini pairs well with the garlic-infused rosé sauce. A bottle of sparkling San Pellegrino water is a good accompaniment. For dessert, there are several moist and fluffy cakes, as well as robust Roma coffee.

Tre Colori started as a specialty food store. You can also purchase fresh pesto, whole-wheat spaghetti, spinach fettuccine, meatballs, slabs of pizza, and biscotti to create an instant supper at home.

Hours: Mon.–Sat. 9 a.m.–8 p.m.
Alcohol: No
Credit cards: Yes
Wheelchair access: One step
Vegetarian friendly: Yes

6544 Somerled (@ Cavendish)
(514) 489-4202
Metro: Villa-Maria, 103 bus

Rôtisserie Italienne

Old-fashioned cheesy chow.

The aroma of melting Mozzarella greets you the moment you open the door of this casual eatery. The décor, like the smell, is pleasantly cheesy—there are red-and-white checkered cloths on the tables and the walls are adorned with plastic chef masks. Place your order at the counter, then decide whether to sit in the dining area for a quick meal or at the counter for an even quicker meal. It gets loud here when it's crowded—which it often is—but the mood is always good-natured. In fact, it's a great place for eavesdropping.

Start off with a green salad or the deep-fried Mozzarella in carozza—square croquettes made with rice or bread. They're only $1.50, and they come topped with a ladle of tomato sauce. The classic pastas are all available here, and the kitchen understands the importance of al dente. Expect to pay about $9.25 for standards like alfredo, pesto, primavera, or vongole, a clam sauce that comes bianco or rosso (white or red).

Almost as popular are the one-person pizzas ($5.75), like the Sicilian, with ham and red peppers, or the Margerita, with Mozzarella and basil. Keep an eye out for daily specials like fried calamari, scaloppine, and mussels. Wine is available in small formats for the solo diner who doesn't want to miss out.

Hours: Mon.–Fri. 11:30 a.m.–11 p.m.
Alcohol: Yes
Credit cards: No
Wheelchair access: No
Vegetarian friendly: Yes

1933 Ste-Catherine W. (@ Towers)
(514) 935-4436
Metro: Guy-Concordia or Atwater

La Strega

Budget pasta in a baroque décor.

This restaurant has carved out a niche for itself in the Gay Village. From the décor to the food on your plate, all the ingredients are here for enjoying a night out without emptying your wallet. The resto's interior displays some vaguely baroque touches, and it's painted in dark colours; the flexible menu allows you to build a meal to suit your budget.

La Strega's strength is its mix-and-match pastas and sauce. Spaghetti, linguine, penne, fettuccine, rigatoni, or fusilli can be paired with napoletana, arrabbiata, primavera, gigi, pesto, or putanesca sauces. Whatever your combo, it'll cost you $6.95. For a couple of bucks more, you can personalize your dish by consulting a list of extras such as sausage, mussels, salmon, shrimp, or Provolone cheese. Panini sandwiches are available for the same price. Oven-baked pastas like cannelloni, lasagne, and manicotti are $8.95.

The table d'hôte, ranging from $6.95 to $15, is a really good deal. It includes soup and a green salad or a small portion of pasta to start—in addition to the complimentary bruschetta. The specials often highlight meats and seafood from the main menu, such as chicken cacciatore, sole provençale, or a number of veal dishes. The veal polignac, for instance, is slathered in a rich cream, cognac, white wine, and mushroom sauce.

Hours: Mon.–Fri. 11:30 a.m.–midnight;
Sat. and Sun. 5 p.m.–midnight
Alcohol: Yes
Credit cards: Yes
Wheelchair access: Yes
Vegetarian friendly: Yes

1477 Ste-Catherine E. (@ Alexandre-de-Sève)
(514) 523-6000
Metro: Beaudry

EATING
grills and gills

Le Galeto

Busy Brazilian churrascaria.

This Brazilian-style rôtisserie caters largely to downtown business types, but it deserves to be discovered by a wider clientele. Opened in summer 2002 by the owners of the more upscale Milsa steakhouse, it offers casual, quick lunches and comfortable counter seating.

The concept here is simple: grilled chicken takes centre stage—literally. Cornish hens are grilled over an open charcoal pit in the middle of the restaurant. You can watch them being basted and roasted—on long, dangerous-looking steel skewers—to crispy, juicy perfection. Then each bird is removed from its skewer, hacked up, and plunked on a pool of brown sauce in the middle of a serving plate. The menu is exclusively table d'hôte (from $10.95 without drink to $14.95 with wine), and your meal includes a garden salad with creamy dressing and a plate of fries with a tempura-like texture. While you chow down, you can eye your mouthwateringly warm and tender dessert being prepared: pineapple browned on the grill, thinly sliced, and sprinkled with cinnamon.

The only other options here are a 12-ounce steak or a generous serving of grilled shrimp. But it's the chicken, and the friendly staff, that will have you coming back for more. Also try a guanará, a Brazilian soft drink made with berries; it's not listed on the menu, but it's the perfect accompaniment.

Hours: Mon.–Fri. 11 a.m.–3 p.m.
Alcohol: Yes
Credit cards: Yes
Wheelchair access: One step
Vegetarian friendly: No

1246 Stanley (@ Ste-Catherine)
(514) 868-0770
Metro: Peel

Marven's

Marvellous man-sized Greek meals.

Stuffed moose heads on the walls, Mythos beer on the tables, and waiters serving enormous helpings of meat—that pretty much sums up this Park Ex paradise. Marven's offers great value for Greek food in crowded and convivial surroundings.

For a real taste of how good the standards can be, begin with the pikilia for one ($6.95). Big enough for two, it features fantastic taramosalata, tzatziki, dolmades (stuffed vine leaves), crispy keftedes (fried meatballs), hot peppers, Feta, and spanakopita and tiropita (filo triangles filled with spinach and cheese, respectively). Alternately, a half-order of deep-fried calamari will do the trick.

For mains, there's gyro, there's souvlaki, and there's the mix-'em-up gyro and souvlaki combo ($9.50), served with Caesar or Greek salad and rice or potatoes. Turn to the slightly pricier back section of the menu for even bigger meals, which start with a fresh Greek salad doused in olive oil, lemon, and oregano. The lamb chops taste like they've just come off your backyard barbecue—if only you knew the secret to the marinade. And the chicken shish kebab, grilled with onion and green pepper, is huge. Dinner at Marven's is more than a meal: it's a challenge to get to the finish line.

Hours: Sun.–Thurs. 11 a.m.–midnight;
Fri. and Sat. 11 a.m.–1 a.m.
Alcohol: Yes
Credit cards: No
Wheelchair access: No
Vegetarian friendly: Limited

---

880 Ball (@ Wiseman)
(514) 277-3625
Metro: Parc

Mommy's Fish and Chips

Old-school fish and chips.

Visiting Mommy's is almost like stepping onto the set of *Coronation Street*—blue-collar grub from the British Isles is alive and well here. Although takeout orders aren't wrapped in newspaper anymore, the constant sizzle of the deep fryer adds an air of authenticity to this fast-food eatery. The décor, however, is limited—the walls are hung with tartan tea towels embellished with images of bagpipes, maps of Scotland, and a poem called "The Wild Hairy Haggis."

Fish-and-chips plates range from $4.25 to $8.95. The catch of choice here is haddock, battered and deep-fried until it takes on a golden hue. Served with a lemon wedge and tartar sauce, it's the ultimate in comfort food. The chips are rough-cut potatoes that retain their form through the most liberal dousing of ketchup and vinegar (no curry sauce, though).

The menu also lists seafood platters of scallops, clams, and deep-fried butterfly shrimp ($8), along with several fish burgers ($3.95). Clam chowder comes steaming hot in styrofoam cups, while the onion rings are so enormous they're more like onion bracelets. Raw oysters from New Brunswick are available in season. There are also several drinks from across the sea, like dandelion and burdock (D&B), ginger beer, and Bass or Newcastle ales.

Hours: Mon.–Wed. 11:30 a.m.–7:30 p.m.;
Thurs. and Fri. 11 a.m.–9 p.m.; Sat. 12 p.m.–9 p.m.
Alcohol: Yes
Credit cards: No
Wheelchair access: Two steps
Vegetarian friendly: No

---

651 de l'Église
(@ Verdun)
(514) 762-1294
Metro: Verdun

3135 Notre-Dame, Lachine
(@ 32nd)
(514) 637-3941
Metro: 195 bus

Peter's Cape Cod

Fresh seafood on the waterfront.

Peter's Cape Cod has been a West Island institution for more than a decade. With its maritime motif, blue-and-white checked tablecloths, and windows overlooking the water, it has the feel of a family restaurant on the boardwalk of a little resort town. Its two terraces open as early as possible in the warm season.

The menu is simple: each day from 11:30 a.m. to 2:30 p.m., a sign that says $8.95 hangs outside. At 2:30 p.m., a staff member turns it over to read $11.95, and it stays that way until closing. Daily soup is usually included, but it's worth the extra $4.95 for the fish chowder with a tomato roux, potatoes, and fresh dill.

The fixed price buys you free access to the riches of the sea, like whole rainbow trout, salmon filet, halibut, dore, B.C. snapper, or mahi-mahi—and the list goes on. Everything is cooked with considerable skill, and it's done pretty much any way you want it. Shrimp, squid, and scallops come breaded, broiled, or fried. All main courses are accompanied by salad and either home fries, baked potato, or rice. The English-style fish and chips consists of cod with a thin coating of batter (cholesterol-free oil is used), chunky Cajun fries, salad, and the house tartar sauce made with mayo, cucumber, and dill. Pastas are available for landlubbers.

Hours: 11:30 a.m.–9:30 p.m. daily; open later on weekends
Alcohol: Yes
Credit cards: Yes
Wheelchair access: Two small steps
Vegetarian friendly: Limited

---

160 Ste-Anne, Ste-Anne-de-Bellevue (@ du Collège)
(514) 457-0081
Metro: Lionel-Groulx, 211 bus

Le Roi du Plateau

Trad Portuguese resto with the will to grill.

The vibe at Le Roi du Plateau is casual and rustic, the servings are plentiful, and the prices are decent. The owner—he of the mighty moustache—used to work at the ever-popular Chez Doval, and he's re-created the Portuguese formula of simple grills here with great success.

To start, try the caldo verde, a national staple—a thick potage of potato and cabbage ($1.50). Other appetizers include camarão ao alho ($6), perfectly cooked shrimp in a tangy garlic butter sauce; tender whole squid rubbed with seasonings ($6.50); and grilled sardines ($4).

The grilled quarter-chicken is a classic at $9; ask for hot sauce to spice it up. Like all the meals, the chicken comes with rice and/or fries and a salad. Twelve bucks gets you a steak served with a fried egg on top and thick fries on the side. The Roi-style mussels ($10), plump, piping hot, and cooked just right, are bathed in a light tomato sauce and served atop a mound of rice. For the full royal experience, order a potent Super Bock beer to wash it all down.

Hours: 5 p.m.–11 p.m. daily
Alcohol: Yes
Credit cards: Yes
Wheelchair access: Two steps
Vegetarian friendly: No

51 Rachel W. (@ Clark)
(514) 844-8393
Metro: Mont-Royal or St-Laurent

Rôtisserie Mavi

Simple pleasures of Portugal.

From the street, the only hint of the excitement within Mavi is a colourful, hand-painted window. Stepping inside is like walking into a neighbourhood snackbar in Portugal. The grill is positioned right beside the front door, and it dominates a room full of activity, sizzling sounds, and smoke. The hungry can only wait and salivate, wondering if the next piece of meat is for them or someone else.

If you've never eaten sardines that didn't come from a can, this is a good place to do it. Other simply grilled seafood selections include cod, calamari, shrimp, salmon, swordfish, and trout ($10 to $11). Mavi is also a haven for meat lovers, who'll find febras (pork), and bitoque (beef), and ribs. A favourite of regulars, the juicy, spicy barbecued chicken ($11.25 for a half, and $8.75 for a breast) is finger-lickin' great. Plates come with thin brown fries and a simple, lightly dressed salad. Sandwiches are available as well, served on crusty rolls.

For a real taste of the other side of the Atlantic, opt for the cod croquettes ($10), hidden at the end of the menu. They're moist and fluffy on the inside, while the outside is lightly deep-fried to crispness. These bullet-shaped wonders are also made with meat or shrimp. Dessert is usually a pineapple mousse.

Hours: Mon.–Wed. 11 a.m.–10 p.m.;
Thurs. and Fri. 11 a.m.–11 p.m.; Sat. 11:30 a.m.–11 p.m.
Alcohol: Yes
Credit cards: No
Wheelchair access: Two steps
Vegetarian friendly: No

5192 Gatineau (@ Jean-Brilliant)
(514) 340-9664
Metro: Côte-des-Neiges

Souvlaki George

Super selection of souvlaki.

This west-end institution makes more kinds of souvlaki than you can shake a stick at. Pita sandwiches are offered with lamb, pork, or chicken brochettes, spiced gyro, loukaniko sausage, or vegetarian-style—with or without Feta cheese. George uses extra-large pita bread that's slapped on the grill for a few seconds to give it a crisscross pattern on the outside; this is filled to the edges with tomatoes, onions, lettuce, and creamy tzatziki. A dinner of classic pork souvlaki with fries and salad is about $8.50; an all-inclusive lunch can be had for $6.

George's moussaka ($7.45), the shepherd's pie of Greece, offers a taste of home cooking. A firm lower crust of sliced potato is layered with delicately spiced ground meat and soft eggplant; this is blanketed with a thick egg-and-cheese béchamel, baked to a custard-like consistency. Served with salad, this dish will cure hunger or homesickness.

The tiny original location in N.D.G. has a homey feel and a blue-and-white colour scheme. On each of the five tables stands a bottle of sparkling water. In warm weather, there's a large terrace within spitting distance of Concordia University. The St-Henri location is more geared towards takeout.

Hours: 11 a.m.–11 p.m. daily; open later for delivery
Alcohol: No
Credit cards: No
Wheelchair access: No
Vegetarian friendly: Limited

6995 Monkland	**749 Atwater**
(@ Coronation)	(@ St-Antoine)
(514) 482-0040	(514) 931-5008
Metro: Vendôme, 105 bus	Metro: Lionel-Groulx

EATING
out of
africa

L'Abidjanaise

A toast to the Ivory Coast.

Specializing in dishes from the Ivory Coast, L'Abidjanaise caters mainly to ex-pat Africans looking for a taste of home. Still, this is a great place for anyone to discover West African cuisine. Tucked away on a residential side street, it pulsates with a warm, upbeat atmosphere, intensified by catchy music videos from the other side of the world.

The menu is divided into sauce-based dishes ($10) and grilled meats ($10 to $12). In the first category, there's mafi chicken, made with peanuts; creamy pépé soupe with tripe or beef; and yassa, a Senegalese concoction of chicken, olives, and onions that's also popular in Côte d'Ivoire. Another option is djoumgblé, a stew composed of cubed beef and flakes of dried fish in a thick, slightly glutinous gravy made with gombo (okra). From the grill, there's chicken or fish—such as a whole plump tilapia with a faint charcoal flavour, topped with thinly sliced onions and tomatoes.

Meals come with a choice of accompaniments, among them attiéké, which is similar to North African couscous, but it's made with cassava instead of semolina; and aloco, fried slices of plantain. There are also some homemade West African drinks to try here: hibiscus juice, called bissape; or a ginger/pineapple beverage called gnamakoudji.

Hours: 5 p.m.–11 p.m. daily
Alcohol: Yes
Credit cards: No
Wheelchair access: Yes
Vegetarian friendly: No

5772 Decelles (@ Côte-Ste-Catherine)
(514) 223-1147
Metro: Côte-Ste-Catherine, 129 bus

Au Bec Fin JRR

Cabbies delight in this Haitian haven.

This Avenue du Parc hole-in-the-wall is a favourite refuelling spot for local taxi drivers, who can often be seen here enjoying inexpensive home-cooked Haitian meals. The daily specials usually feature seafood, pintade (guinea hen), and stews; these are served with soup or salad for $8 to $13. The red snapper is steamed whole, adorned with sliced onions and red peppers, and presented with a thin, tasty sauce. Alternately, select a bowl of dense, aromatic stew and personalize it with your choice of veggies—like eggplant, spinach, or mirliton (chayote), along with diced carrot, onion, cabbage, beans, and parsley stems.

Meals are accompanied by Haitian-style bananes pesées—plantains flattened into discs and fried to a semi-crunchy texture. You are also given a choice of plain white rice or riz collé, a delicious Creole staple made with long-grain rice, kidney beans, and flecks of chili.

This informal resto is often packed to the rafters at lunchtime, and the atmosphere can be a little daunting—the cabbies tend to talk shop at the top of their lungs, competing with the TV. But you can get a takeout order, find a taxi (no problem here), and make it home while the food's still hot!

Hours: Mon.–Sat. noon–7 p.m.
Alcohol: No
Credit cards: No
Wheelchair access: Yes
Vegetarian friendly: No

5607 du Parc (@ St-Viateur)
(514) 278-6134
Metro: Parc, 80 bus

Les Délices de l'Île Maurice

Mauritius for the armchair traveller.

The cuisine of Mauritius, like its history, is a real stewpot of influences. This island in the Indian Ocean was colonized by the Portuguese, Dutch, French, and British. Throw into the mix the fact that its residents are of African, Indian, and Chinese descent, and you get one spicy mélange. Les Délices de l'Île Maurice evokes this tropical paradise to great effect in the middle of Verdun, thanks in part to the quirky presence of owner/chef Sylvestre—a large Asian man in shorts and a V-necked butcher's apron who talks like de Gaulle.

Barely have you nestled into a seat when you are presented with a plate of yummy fried cabbage, accompanied by four homemade sauces—mint, tomato, garlic, and chili pepper. This is quickly followed by a dal soup served with a lemon wedge. Next, be prepared to mix and match meats and seafood with various sauces: Créole, Cajun, curry, tomato, or saffron. The lamb curry, for instance, is exquisitely tender. The huge seared scallops topped with tomato, onion, peppers, and ginger are just as delicious. Dishes come with rice and salad. Everything is so fresh, aromatic, and exciting here that you'll find it hard to go wrong—especially since your memorable meal costs less than $10.

Hours: 5 p.m.–10 p.m. daily
Alcohol: BYOB
Credit cards: No
Wheelchair access: Yes
Vegetarian friendly: No

272 Hickson (@ Wellington)
(514) 768-6023
Metro: de l'Église

Jamaica Way

Cool jerk and other reggae recipes.

Jamaica Way is a colourful, vaguely haphazard space where you'll encounter a chilled vibe, reggae tunes, and inexpensive Caribbean food. If you like jerk chicken, you'll be happy here. The skin is blackened to form a crisp casing that seals in moisture, and the meat is slathered with a distinctive sauce flavoured with allspice, potent Scotch bonnets, and thyme. Selections are thoughtfully offered in two sizes: $6 for small, and $8 for large. Like all the meals, the jerk comes with red peas (kidney beans), rice, and plantains that are puffy, soft, and sweet like caramel. You can also get a chewy-gooey dumpling topped with tomato sauce to go with it.

The salt fish and calalloo is equally delicious ($7 or $10). The dish is made of dried, salted cod simmered with onions, tomatoes, a hint of spice, and chopped calalloo, a vegetable that's like a cross between spinach and collard greens. You can also get your salt fish with ackee, a combo that's often referred to as Jamaica's national dish.

On the menu board you'll also see oxtail stew, red snapper, kingfish, and curried goat. Alternately, for a quick meal you can hold in your hand, order patties filled with vegetables, chicken, or beef—they're only a buck each. Desserts include peanut sugar cake, coconut sugar cake, coconut balls, and jackass cookies.

Hours: Tues. and Wed. 9 a.m.–10 p.m.;
Thurs.–Sat. 9 a.m.–11 p.m.
Alcohol: No
Credit cards: No
Wheelchair access: No
Vegetarian friendly: No

4961-B Queen Mary (@ Snowdon)
(514) 343-5375
Metro: Snowdon

Jardin du Cari

Rotis and curries from Guyana.

With its Caribbean rotis, East Indian curries, and Asian chow meins, the menu at Jardin du Cari summarizes the ethnic influences at play in the tiny South American nation of Guyana. The original owners of this low-key Mile End establishment moved away in 2001, leaving the business in the capable hands of relatives, so its fans can still get a friendly fix of homemade food.

One special favourite is the rotis ($5.50 and up)—big pockets of unleavened bread bursting with goat, boneless chicken, shrimp, or chickpea and potato fillings that have been simmered in spices. Rotis are offered with or without stewed pumpkin, which adds a sweeter, thicker taste. Round out your meal with an order of potato balls ($2), and enjoy their hot, lemony aroma. For a bigger spread, request one of the curry plates, which come with rice, plantains, potatoes, and salad. These pungently flavoured stews, ladled over rice, are made with the same meats as the rotis, and there's also a vegetarian option ($6.55 to $9.75).

At Jardin du Cari, there's a bottle opener on every table. The reason for this becomes apparent when you see the list of West Indian colas in flavours like pineapple, sorrel, peanut punch, and a sweet and sassy ginger beer that catches delightfully in your throat.

Hours: Tues.–Thurs. noon–9:30 p.m.; Fri. and Sat. noon–11 p.m.; Sun. 5 p.m.–9 p.m.
Alcohol: Yes
Credit cards: No
Wheelchair access: No
Vegetarian friendly: Yes

21 St-Viateur W. (@ Clark)
(514) 495-0565
Metro: St-Laurent, 55 bus

Kamela

Couscous, briks, and more Tunisian treats.

Not only does Kamela dish up some of the most inexpensive couscous in town, but it also provides a charming space in which to consume it. Decorated with patterned cushions, coloured tiles, and North African curios, it makes you want to take your shoes off and linger—although delivery service is available in the Plateau area.

For a taste of Tunisian street food, try one of the 10 briks ($8.50 with salad). These pastry pockets, often stuffed with egg, make a light meal or a shared appetizer. Fillings include spinach and Feta, spicy ground beef and onions, and even snails. The Kamela Brik is jam-packed with artichokes, asparagus, olives, tomatoes, and Feta, while the seafood version contains shrimp, clams, and mock crab tinged with garlic.

Couscous is another specialty here. Plates are for one or two people, with prices starting at $7.50 (taxes included) for a single vegetarian order. Meat combos—featuring merguez, chicken, brochettes, or lamb chops—are a good way to go (from $11.95). Dishes come with a generous serving of a sauce of vegetables, chickpeas, raisins, and hot harissa.

There's another side to Kamela's personality: it's also a pizza parlour! Standard toppings are available, along with more exotic variations, like Feta, goat cheese, and merguez.

Hours: Mon.–Thurs. 11 a.m.–2 p.m., 4 p.m.–11 p.m.;
Fri.–Sun. 4 p.m.–11 p.m.
Alcohol: No
Credit cards: No; Interac accepted
Wheelchair access: No
Vegetarian friendly: Yes

1227 Marie-Anne E. (@ de la Roche)
(514) 528-0881
Metro: Mont-Royal, 97 or 11 bus

Ma's Place

Home-cooked Caribbean classics.

This relaxed N.D.G. eatery, with a second location in Ville St-Laurent, serves huge portions of rib-sticking soul food at reasonable prices. You've got to love a place that has something on the menu for 25 cents; at Ma's, that's the going rate for a fried dumpling or a plantain to accompany your meal. And for less than $2 you can get a piece of jerk chicken added to your plate for good measure.

You won't need the extras, though, as even the small portions ($7.50 to $8) are king-sized here. House dishes include stewed beef, curried beef, curried goat, and the popular jerk. The curried chicken, simmered in a pungent sauce, falls off the bone. The oxtail stew in thick brown gravy is another classic—if you don't mind working the meat off the bone. Mains are served with your choice of red beans and rice or plain white rice, plus a basic iceberg salad. There are also several types of fish, including red snapper ($12) cooked three ways: fried, steamed, or brown stewed. Rotis, including vegetarian, are also sold at this cozy hideaway ($4.50).

Hours: Mon.–Wed. 11 a.m.–9 p.m.; Thurs.–Sat. 24 hours; Sun. 11 a.m.–8 p.m.
Alcohol: No
Credit cards: No
Wheelchair access: No
Vegetarian friendly: Limited

5889 Sherbrooke W.
(@ Clifton)
(514) 487-7488
Metro: Vendôme, 105 bus

850 Décarie
(@ de l'Église)
(514) 744-2011
Metro: du Collège

EATING
novelty
nosh

L'Auberge du Dragon Rouge

Medieval madness.

What must the neighbours have thought when a strange inn-keeper took over the house next door and transformed it into a medieval tavern? The décor is decidedly rough-and-tumble, and the atmosphere is consistently boisterous. A band of troubadours and serving wenches in period costume shout at patrons in Olde French, burst into song, and generally behave like rabble-rousers.

The menu delves deep into the past for inspiration. The chicken with sauce saupiquet ($12.95), for instance, dates back to 1197 A.D., and it's flavoured with a woodsy combination of ginger, nutmeg, smoked lard, and saffron. Other historical dishes, like boar simmered with chestnuts and cider, are a little more expensive. For a budget option, try a delicious hamburger—first created in Hamburg in 971—of chicken, ostrich, boar and Brie, or venison and goat cheese. The Ogre ($9 for a medium-sized) is a beef patty topped with Mozzarella, bacon, mushrooms, peppers, and onions. Fans of fries will revel in two kinds: the spicy Saxonne and the chiplike Petite Pétàque.

No self-respecting medieval tavern would be caught dead without drink, and there are plenty of craft beers to try here. Also of interest: hydromels—honey wines, which the Druids used during fertility rituals. Oyez, oyez, as they say!

Hours: Mon.–Wed. 11:30 a.m.–10 p.m.; Thurs. and Fri. 11:30 a.m.–11 p.m.; Sat. 4:30 p.m.–11 p.m.; Sun. 4:30 p.m.–10 p.m.
Alcohol: Yes
Credit cards: No; Interac accepted
Wheelchair access: Through terrace
Vegetarian friendly: Limited

8874 Lajeunesse (@ Emile-Journault)
(514) 858-5711
Metro: Crémazie

Cabaret Les Amazones

A feast for the eyes and the stomach.

Sure, it's a little distracting to be digging into dinner while someone's wiggling the wild stuff a few yards away, but strip clubs can be great venues for budget meals. And these establishments are not just for gentlemen—anyone's welcome, as long as they're 18 or over, of course. While many downtown clubs no longer have kitchen service, this N.D.G. cabaret is still cooking. Pay the entry fee, usually a nominal one, and you're in like Flynn! The buffet awaits.

Although there's a full menu that lists the usual suspects—hamburgers, souvlaki, chicken wings—the buffet, with its decent selection of hot and cold dishes (11 a.m. to 7 p.m. on weekdays), delivers the best possible bang for your buck: it's on the house. The food isn't going to win any awards for imagination or quality, but it's free, so who's complaining?

Les Amazones is located on a strip of low-rent motels, downstairs from Picasso's, a popular all-day/all-night family-style diner. The club occupies a cavernous space with one large central stage and two smaller ones. The dancing Amazones are lovely ladies in their twenties to mid-thirties, some of whom are quite acrobatic.

Hours: Mon.–Sat. 11 a.m.–3 a.m.; Sun. 7 p.m.–3 a.m.
Alcohol: Yes
Credit cards: Yes
Wheelchair access: No
Vegetarian friendly: Not really

6820 St-Jacques (@ Cavendish)
(514) 484-8695
Metro: Vendôme, 90 bus

Café Ramses

Egyptian exotica.

Café Ramses is an oasis of Egyptian exotica on the South Shore. Sheeshas are the big attraction here—elaborate glass and brass pipes filled with water and aromatic tobacco ($6.10). Also known as hookahs, they originated in Turkey more than five centuries ago. The enticing flavours they offer come from a gelatinous mixture of jam, molasses, and tobacco, and they include apple, honey, mint, grape, melon, pistachio, black licorice, apricot, cappuccino, and fakhfakhina, a mix of exotic fruits and whipped cream. Reclining on cushions or settled in comfy armchairs, Ramses patrons puff away on their sheeshas, chat, and take in the occasional belly dance show.

Sheeshas go well with tea, served here in little gold-rimmed glasses with matching saucers, Arab-style. Among the varieties: Chinese cherry, walnut, black currant, orange flower, hibiscus, and a house creation similar to chai.

Ramses also serves light meals. For $3.50, you can get stuffed vine leaves, baba gannouj, or hummus. One of the best snacks is definitely the Bruschetta Oriental ($4.50), a round of toasted pita slathered with yogurt, cilantro, and minced jalapeños and topped with a salsa of extra-fresh tomatoes dotted with garlic and herbs. Hamburgers ($7.95) come with dark, meaty fries and paprika-dusted mayo.

Hours: Sun. and Thurs. 2 p.m.–midnight; Mon. and Wed. 5 p.m.–midnight; Fri. and Sat. 2 p.m.–2 a.m.
Alcohol: Yes
Credit cards: Yes
Wheelchair access: Two steps
Vegetarian friendly: Yes

8500 Taschereau W., Brossard (near Pont Champlain)
(450) 923-4659

Do-Ré-Mi

Ballroom blitz!

Back in the good ol' days, dancehalls were a dime a dozen. People would flock to these places because there, under one roof, they could enjoy a whole night of entertainment, eating, and exercise. Do-Ré-Mi provides this type of old-style dinner-and-dance experience in a glitzy, if not very ritzy, ballroom.

There is a set menu for each soirée; you can find out what it is via a recorded phone message. Expect the basic cookbook fare, like leg of lamb, chicken cacciatore, beef teriyaki, veal Parmigiana, pasta trio, roast beef, or stuffed cabbage. If nothing on the menu appeals, you can always fall back on the always-available spaghetti with tomato sauce. Dessert, like a super-fake Black Forest cake, is included. Customers eat off plastic trays under globe lanterns. Clearly, the food is very basic—and most of it is very easy to chew. But where else can you fill your tummy and witness a crazy dance-athon for as little as $12?

Most of the regulars are in their golden years, but that doesn't stop them—or you—from getting down and dirty to the music. Flashing neon signs announce the upcoming dance style: foxtrot, triple swing, mambo, cha-cha, tango, or rumba. For aspiring ballroom dancers, it's a chance to spin around the floor; for seniors, it's a chance to party like it's 1949.

Hours: Wed. 6 p.m.–11:30 p.m.; Fri. 6 p.m.–1:30 a.m.;
Sat. 6:30 p.m.–2 a.m., Sun. 4 p.m.–midnight
Alcohol: Yes
Credit cards: No
Wheelchair access: No
Vegetarian friendly: No

505 Bélanger (@ St-Vallier)
(514) 274-5456
Metro: Jean-Talon

Gibeau Orange Julep

Taste the nectar of Montreal's giant roadside orange.

Undoubtedly Montreal's most distinctive roadside attraction, Gibeau Orange Julep has been beckoning to those in search of sustenance for more than 60 years. The giant orange dome near the Décarie Expressway was built in the 1940s by a gastronomic visionary named Hermas Gibeau. His intention was to live in the three-storey sphere with his wife and kids while dispensing his foamy citrus beverage from the ground-level counter. Today, the sweet, creamy, frothy drink is piped down from the top of the structure and served in small to extra-large formats ($1.73 to $7.25).

The menu is a fast-food cornucopia: hotdogs, pogos, hamburgers, fries, and onion rings. In 2002, some new items were added: a salmon burger with a slightly crunchy exterior and a moist interior ($6 with fries, slaw, and a medium julep); and a tasty roast beef sandwich made with thinly sliced meat, fried onions, and melted cheese ($3.95).

A visit to the Orange Julep is filled with nostalgic charm. Waitresses on roller skates will zoom over to take your order through the car window, or you can grab a seat at one of the outdoor picnic tables. For more of that old-time feeling, stop by on a Wednesday night in summer, when classic car enthusiasts show off their wheels.

Hours: 24/7; more restricted in winter
Alcohol: No
Credit cards: No; Interac accepted
Wheelchair access: Yes
Vegetarian friendly: Limited

7700 Décarie (@ Paré)
(514) 738-7486
Metro: Namur

Jardin Tiki

Polynesian paradise for kitsch lovers.

Jardin Tiki is about as close as you'll get to the set of *Fantasy Island* in Montreal. You even have to cross a bridge—over a pond inhabited by live turtles—to reach your table. A throwback to the Polynesian craze that swept North America in the fifties and sixties, the restaurant is full of Easter Island statuettes and shell lamps, and ukuleles play on the soundtrack.

The enormous all-you-can-eat buffet ranges from $9 to $14.95, depending on the day and time. More than 30 hot-tray selections blend suburban Chinese fare with office-party food, but the supply is plentiful. Help yourself to spring rolls, carve-your-own roast beef, spareribs, baby back ribs, sautéed broccoli and beef, pineapple chicken, noodles, onion rings, roasted potatoes, Asian dumplings, wonton soup, and spicy chicken with red peppers. Plus: cocktail weenies wrapped in bacon—redundant but tasty! Refresh yourself after this massive cholesterol hit with a trip to the salad bar. Then head off to the dessert section, where you'll find a self-serve soft ice cream dispenser—a childhood dream come true!

Dip into the impressive assortment of tropical cocktails ($5.50 to $7), including Mai Tais, Scorpions, Bolos, and the Aku-Aku, which comes in a coconut shell that's been run through the dishwasher a few times too many.

Hours: Mon.–Fri. 11:30 a.m.–2:30 p.m., 4:30 p.m.–10 p.m.; Fri. and Sat. 11:30 a.m.–1 a.m.
Alcohol: Yes
Credit cards: Yes
Wheelchair access: Yes
Vegetarian friendly: Barely

5300 Sherbrooke E. (@ de l'Assomption)
(514) 254-4173
Metro: Assomption

02 Oasis Oxygène

Breathe easier at this oxygen bar.

Oxygen bars became somewhat of a fixture in major cities and airports during the late 1990s. They were places where the world-weary could go to get a breath of fresh air. Montreal's 02 Oasis Oxygène opened in the hot and smoggy summer of 2002 in a space that combines natural elements with space-age style. Long strips of wood curve up from the floor to meet the ceiling, creating a rib-cage effect, and round booths are illuminated with a deep-blue hue.

02 is essentially a walk-in spa, offering a condensed pampering experience for people who don't have the time, money, or patience to spend a day indulging their minds, bodies, and spirits. Ten minutes of air supply costs $7 ($7.95 for 15 minutes; $12 for 20 minutes), and you can even select a scent—like jasmine, witch hazel, or rosemary. At the inhaling stations, the superoxygenated jet is conducted up your nose through plastic tubing, hospital-style, and it's supposed to aid digestion and respiration, boost stamina, and soothe emotional stress and headaches. Add a 10-minute in-chair massage for $12, or put them both together for $16.

Healthy snacks are also available here—sandwiches and salads made with yummy ingredients like grilled chicken, chèvre, and portobello mushrooms. There's also a lineup of energy-restoring beverages.

Hours: 11 a.m.–midnight daily
Alcohol: No
Credit cards: Visa; Interac accepted
Wheelchair access: One step
Vegetarian friendly: Yes

4059 St-Laurent (@ Duluth)
(514) 284-1196
Metro: St-Laurent or Mont-Royal

EATING
on the
run

Adonis

Middle Eastern multi-culti madness.

For grocery shopping ethnic-style, nothing beats Adonis: it's the king of the Middle Eastern markets. Grab a bag of pita and pair it with one of the wonderful dips: hummus, baba gannouj, labneh, mousakahah (eggplant, chickpeas, and tomatoes), or moudardarah (lentils, rice, onions, and spices). The baked-goods section is filled with honey-infused desserts and savoury pastries: baklava, fatayer, sambousek, and kebbeh—bulgur balls bulging with sea-soned beef and pine nuts.

Adonis is also barbecue central. For an instant meal, call ahead and reserve a roasted chicken ($6.49), which comes wrapped in pita, with creamy garlic sauce. It's a delight of tender meat and crackling skin. For the home grill, there's uncooked shish taouk, shawarma, and souvlaki, along with pure beef sausages like soujouk, merguez, and loukaniko flavoured with orange essence.

This is also a one-stop shop for exotic produce, whether it's almonds in the shell, fresh dates, figs, baladi cucumbers, or enormous green fava beans. Nearby, you'll find dried lemons, bright-pink marinated turnip, 12 kinds of olives, vine leaves, filo, and halvah aplenty. The frozen-food section is equally intriguing; here you'll discover artichokes, coriander, okra, and only-in-Egypt ingredients like moloukhia, a leafy vegetable similar to spinach but with an aroma reminiscent of henna.

Hours: Mon. and Tues. 9 a.m.–7 p.m.; Wed. 9 a.m.–8 p.m.; Thurs. and Fri. 9 a.m.–9 p.m.; Sat. and Sun. 9 a.m.–6 p.m.
Credit cards: No; Interac accepted
Wheelchair access: Yes
Vegetarian friendly: Yes

2001 Sauvé W.
(@ l'Acadie)
(514) 382-8606
Metro: Côte-Vertu, 121 bus

4601 des Sources, Pierrefonds
(@ Pierrefonds)
(514) 685-5050
Metro: du Collège, 214 bus

Coco Rico

The best barbecued chicken, ribs, and pork on the Main.

This corner storefront keeps it simple, and it's been doing so amid the hustle and bustle of the Main for a quarter century. Passersby stop to watch the workers behind the counter as they slice and serve some of the best barbecued meats in town. If you're lucky, you'll be able to nab a stool here, but you'll probably be getting your order to go.

There are three sandwich choices, all served on delicious firm-but-squishy Portuguese rolls. Ham goes for $2.95; sliced pork dripping with juice is a real mouthful for $3.95; the divinely grilled chicken is $3.45. Spices and sauce are optional, but the orange gravy seeping into the bread is part of the fun. For a fork-and-knife meal, try the quarter-chicken and rib combo at $7.99.

You could also choose a salad—macaroni, coleslaw, carrot—but who're you kidding? You don't want to miss the roasted new potatoes—they may be small in size, but they're huge on taste and delightfully crusty; a small order is 95 cents and a large is $2.95. For dessert, get some natas—Portuguese custard tarts, deep brown on top. They're better than a chocolate bar and cost only 85 cents.

Hours: 9 a.m.–10 p.m. daily
Credit cards: No; Interac accepted
Wheelchair access: Yes
Vegetarian friendly: No

3907 St-Laurent (@ Napoléon)
(514) 849-5554
Metro: St-Laurent, 55 bus

Hoàng Oanh

Vietnamese submarine sandwiches.

One bite of bánh mì, and it's easy to see why these Vietnamese submarine sandwiches have developed something of cult following. Combining elements from the cuisines of the various cultures that occupied Vietnam over the years—China, Japan, France, maybe even the U.S.—they are among the best lunch foods around.

Into a length of dense, baguette-like bread, sliced before your eyes, goes your choice of fillings, all of which are laid out behind the counter on immaculate little trays. Meats include chicken, pork, or beef, in grilled, shredded, pâté, or cold-cut form. Then strips of lightly pickled carrot and radish, fresh cilantro sprigs, and seasoned mayo are added. The interplay of contrasting flavours and textures is what makes these sandwiches so different and refreshing. Hot green peppers, guaranteed to bring tears to your eyes, are optional.

Montreal's bánh mì stands tend to be small and jam-packed with all sorts of premade dishes in clear plastic containers. Many foods are completely unrecognizable, and the staff can't always find the words to explain what they are. Look for marinated tofu, taro, pork dumplings with sliced black mushrooms, and flaky puff pastries. However, beware the appealingly coloured agar-based desserts: they don't taste like they look!

Hours: Sat.–Wed. 10 a.m.–8 p.m.; Thurs. and Fri. 10 a.m.–9 p.m.
Credit cards: No; Interac accepted
Wheelchair access: No
Vegetarian friendly: Yes

1071 St-Laurent
(@ René-Lévesque)
(514) 954-0053
Metro: Place-d'Armes

7178 St-Denis
(@ Jean-Talon)
(514) 271-8668
Metro: Jean-Talon

Saum-mon

Atlantic salmon, in every way, shape, and form.

Part of the specialty food shop trend on the thriving Mont-Royal strip, Saum-mon's flagship store smokes, sells, and serves Atlantic salmon on the premises. While shopping for fishy fixings, you can also peruse the on-site fish-motif merchandise.

Light meals are offered daily for $6.95, mostly to go. The price includes a small soup and your choice of entrée. The bagel with salmon tartare is a nice alternative to gravlax; the very fresh flesh is sprinkled with lemon juice, which "cooks" it. This selection comes with a basic salad of curly lettuce and rings of Spanish onion. The ravioli salad is composed of greens and huge pasta wontons stuffed with a herbed salmon mixture. A tasting plate ($7.95) offers you the chance to sample various salmon preparations: poached, raw, moussed, and rolled with seaweed; it also includes a generous portion of smoked salmon and capers.

There's a catering side to this business—serve-it-at-home customers can order hot and cold canapés, soups, and precooked meals. Finally, a note to fishermen: if you've just caught one "this big," the people at Saum-mom will smoke, slice, fillet, or freeze it for you, just as if they'd reeled it in themselves!

Hours: Mon.–Wed. 11 a.m.–6:30 p.m.;
Thurs. and Fri. 11 a.m.–9 p.m.; Sat. 10 a.m.–5:30 p.m.;
Sun. noon–5:30 p.m.
Credit cards: Yes
Wheelchair access: Yes
Vegetarian friendly: No

1318 Mont-Royal E.
(@ de Lanaudière)
(514) 526-1116
Metro: Mont-Royal, 97 bus

345 Victoria
(@ Sherbrooke)
(514) 488-0116
Metro: Vendôme, 90 bus

Sushi au Volant

The original takeout sushi.

In the days before there were fast-food sushi places on every corner, there was Sushi au Volant. Some even say it's the best sushi in the city—no small claim, considering the number of places that now offer the Japanese staple. This cute and impeccably clean shop is strictly to go—the hungry sit on a little wooden bench awaiting their takeout.

Order à la carte, or choose one of the fixed-price combos, like the 12-piece matsu for one person ($14.50). Nigiri (fish on rice) or sashimi (just fish) selections range from $3.75 to $4.75 for two pieces, and they include two kinds of tuna, eel, salmon, amaebi (sweet shrimp), tobiko (flying-fish roe), hotategai (scallop), and shime saba (marinated mackerel). Horo maki are simple, smaller rolls that usually contain a single ingredient—such as cucumber, pickle, tuna, or avocado; they start at $3 for six pieces. Maki—California, Montreal, or Boston rolls, for instance—pack in more ingredients and start at $5 for four pieces. However, even the simplest sushi is treated with reverence here.

Weekday orders should be placed about five hours in advance, and a full day's notice should be given on Fridays and Saturdays. While that requires some planning on the diner's part, it's also an indication that everything here is incredibly fresh.

Hours: Tues.–Fri. 11:30 a.m.–7 p.m.;
Sat. 11:30 a.m.–6 p.m.
Credit cards: No; Interac accepted
Wheelchair access: No
Vegetarian friendly: Limited

---

519 Rachel E. (@ de Chateaubriand)
(514) 523-1085
Metro: Sherbrooke

Tortilleria Maya

Mexican snacks from a tortilla factory.

This place is a bona fide tortilla factory. It's filled with gleaming machines, and its shelves are stocked with products made on the premises—like corn-flour tortillas, saucer-sized tostadas, nachos of various kinds, and chicharrón (salted pork rind). Cans of chipotle, adobe, and jalapeño peppers are also sold here.

Going to Tortilleria Maya means going straight to the source— the food is as fresh as it gets. There are just a few items on offer, and they're really more suitable as a satisfying snack, but you can build a meal out of them. The burritos ($3) are excellent, bursting with rich, creamy refried beans, well-seasoned ground beef, chunks of onion and tomato, fresh coriander, and hot salsa if you want it (you want it). The chicken version is just as good, filled with the same accoutrements and loosely cut white meat. Melted cheese oozes delightfully into the folds of the bread.

The taco ($1.50) is presented in true Mexican style, on a soft shell, and, in the case of the beef, the meat is cut in chunks. Nachos are offered in small or large formats ($3.99 or $4.99); orders comprise corn chips with melted cheese over a bean and beef mixture seasoned with a dash of hot pepper. Muy autentica!

Hours: Mon.–Wed. 10 a.m.–6 p.m.; Thurs. and Fri. 10 a.m.–8 p.m.; Sat. 10 a.m.–5 p.m.
Credit cards: No
Wheelchair access: One step
Vegetarian friendly: Limited

5274 St-Laurent (@ St-Viateur)
(514) 495-0606
Metro: St-Laurent, 55 bus/Laurier, 51 bus

William J. Walter

Gourmet Euro-dogs.

This master saucissier has become a fixture in Montreal's public markets, favoured for its top-grade gourmet links, pâtés, cold cuts, sauerkraut, and mustards. The charming shops of this franchise successfully blend Euro style with Québécois down-to-earthiness. The quality is consistently high, and the products are low in fat and rich in taste.

There are about 50 types of sausage to choose from. For something smoky, try the Acapulco, Mexican, Italian, or Louisiana links. On the spicy side, there's Cajun chicken and Portuguese chorizo. Gourmet creations include apple and bacon, truffle and port, blue cheese and leek, and pecan and maple. Classics like weisswurst, bratwurst, and breakfast sausage are also good. The house dog is the William, which is offered mild, spicy, or extra-spicy, plus the William Suisse, made with Emmenthal cheese.

In summer, William J. Walter sets up an outdoor barbecue booth. European sandwiches are $3.75, cold-cut sandwiches are $4.25, and they make great hold-in-your-hand treats. Otherwise, you can work your own magic with them at home on the barbecue or in the kitchen (boil uncooked sausages before grilling). William J. Walter has other locations: on Monkland in N.D.G. and on Mont-Royal in the Plateau.

Hours: Mon.–Wed. 9 a.m.–6 p.m.; Thurs. and Fri. 9 a.m.–8 p.m.; Sat. 9 a.m.–6 p.m.; Sun. 9 a.m.–5 p.m.
Credit cards: No; Interac accepted
Wheelchair access: One step
Vegetarian friendly: No

Marché Atwater
(south end, indoors)
(514) 933-4070
Metro: Lionel-Groulx

Marché Jean-Talon
(south side)
(514) 279-0053
Metro: Jean-Talon

EATING something sweet

Bilboquet

You'll scream for this haute ice cream.

Often the scene of block-long lineups, this Outremont institution elevates ice cream to an art form. It's all handmade, and it's denser and far tastier than the usual store-bought variety. Selecting a flavour is fun: try one with a quirky name, like Cacaophonie, Caramel Bronzé, Caraméléo, Choco-Choc; or go for chocolate-orange, praline, or pistachio. But even a flavour as run-of-the-mill as vanilla is spectacular here. The maple syrup ice cream is a real treat, and, of course, it's made with the real thing. A mini cup is $1.50, a single is $2.60 (you can combine two half scoops), and a double is $4.10.

Bilboquet also whips up a variety of sorbets, a good option for the diet conscious, because this sorbet contains 70 percent fruit and no fat at all. The flavours are just as mouthwatering: blackcurrant, lemon, strawberry, raspberry, pear, mango, coconut, litchi, and grapefruit. Tropical mixes, banana splits, ice cream sandwiches, milkshakes, and crazy cakes are also available.

Although its raison d'être is ice cream, Bilboquet does offer light snacks for those puritans who can't take their dessert without a spot of lunch or dinner. Quiches and salads are served, as are sandwiches on baguette, bagel, or croissant, with fillings like pâté de campagne; ham, cheese, and béchamel; or Hungarian salami.

Hours: 7 a.m.–midnight daily in summer; closes earlier in off-season; closed January through mid-March
Alcohol: No
Credit cards: No
Wheelchair access: Yes

1311 Bernard W. (@ Outremont)
(514) 276-0414
Metro: Outremont

Claude Postel

Luscious French pastries and chocolates.

Claude Postel, in Old Montreal, is a true French café from floor to ceiling. The pale-yellow walls, dark tables, gilded mirrors, and sombre paintings lend a classy and timeless air to the place. The big attraction, though, is a huge glass display case in which pastries of every permutation glisten, inviting you to make an afternoon pit stop.

People make special trips here just for the crème brûlée ($1.85), offered in vanilla, coffee, and—best of all—maple syrup versions. There are also tiny tartelettes ($2.90) made with all kinds of fruit; the lemon meringue is a standout. Among the individual-sized pastries, sumptuous pairings include pear and caramel, apricot and nougat, and mango and chocolate. A creation called White Pearl is a fluffy mixture of cheese mousse and white chocolate adorned with glazed strawberries, grapes, orange, and pineapple.

The shop also dispenses handmade ice creams and sorbets, as well as gourmet chocolates, many with a semisweet base, with luscious fillings like Cointreau, cherry, and praline.

Light daily meals, in addition to salads and sandwiches on a variety of exquisitely fresh breads, are quite affordable. For about $6.50, you get soup, a main course, and salad. If you're looking for something more substantial, try the early-evening table d'hôte, starting at $14.

Hours: Mon. and Tues. 7 a.m.–7 p.m.; Wed.–Fri.
7 a.m.–9 p.m.; Sat. 9 a.m.–9 p.m.; Sun. 9 a.m.–5 p.m.
Alcohol: Yes
Credit cards: Yes
Wheelchair access: Yes

75 Notre-Dame W. (@ Place-d'Armes)
(514) 844-8750
Metro: Place-d'Armes

Duc de Lorraine

Croissants, cookies, chocolates, cheeses, and creamy confections.

This quaint establishment is part eatery, part working bakery. It has the feel of the kind of family business you'd find in France—and, indeed, it was founded in the 1950s by a pastry pro from Lorraine. Stop by for a good dose of coffee and some of the best croissants in town. Made on the spot, they're extra-fresh and buttery au bout! The ones filled with almond paste are also delicious ($1.95 to go, or $2.25 to eat in).

Duc de Lorraine's stellar array of desserts includes pop-in-your-mouth petit fours, chocolate éclairs, and cream-based pastries like raspberry-chocolate, mocha, and St-Honoré. Their line of delicate cookies ($3.60 a dozen) features chocolate-dipped biarritz, cigarette rolls, orange tuiles, ultra-thin contesses, and frosted galettes. Other specialties—glazed chestnuts, fruits marinated in brandy, cakes, truffles, and chocolates—make wonderful gifts.

For lunch, grab a seat at one of the 15 or so tables. The list of light meals includes a ham and cheese sandwich on croissant ($3.95, hot or cold), croque-monsieur, excellent quiche, and a vol-au-vent filled with béchamel, chicken, and mushrooms. In addition, the shop offers a variety of imported cheeses, pâté sandwiches on French bread, and mousses made with salmon or lobster and shrimp.

Hours: Mon.–Thurs. 8:30 a.m.–6 p.m.;
Fri. 8:30 a.m.–6:30 p.m.; Sat. and Sun. 8:30 a.m.–5 p.m.
Alcohol: No
Credit cards: Yes
Wheelchair access: No

5002 Côte-des-Neiges (@ Queen Mary)
(514) 731-4128
Metro: Côte-des-Neiges or Snowdon

Kilo

Creative cake emporium.

Kilo celebrates gluttony with funky flair. This bakery-café made its mark during the cheesecake craze of the eighties, and it's never stopped producing delectable desserts. Watching customers peer into the display case, it might occur to you that this could be where the expression "like a kid in a candy store" originated (in fact, Kilo also sells bulk candy from big glass jars).

The toughest thing about eating here is deciding which kind of cake, torte, or pie to indulge in ($3.65 to $5.25 a piece). Chocolate freaks should beware the Avalanche (five layers of chocolate cake with chocolate butter-cream filling), the seven-layer Bart Simpson, and the fudgy Roche Noire. Other favourites include a Skor bar mousse made with chocolate, butter toffee, and almonds; a divinely iced carrot cake made with pineapple, raisins, and walnuts; and King Kong banana cake concocted of English cream and white chocolate shavings. The three-berry pie is a slightly tart treat, while the cheesecakes are smoothly satisfying.

For a den of sin, Kilo offers surprisingly healthy meals. Check out the line of fun sandwiches, especially the inventive croques with vegetables, chicken, roast beef, or tuna, topped with melted cheese and served with salad.

Hours: Mon. 5 p.m.–midnight; Tues.–Thurs. 10:30 a.m.–midnight; Fri. 10:30 a.m.–2 a.m.; Sat. 1 p.m.–2 a.m.; Sun. 1 p.m.–midnight
Alcohol: Yes
Credit cards: Yes
Wheelchair access: One step

1495 Ste-Catherine E.
(@ Alexandre-de-Sève)
(514) 596-3933
Metro: Papineau

5206 St-Laurent
(@ Fairmount)
(514) 277-5039
Metro: St-Laurent, 55 bus

New Navarino

Cheap treats in a Greek coffee shop.

Navarino functions primarily as a Greek bakery, and often their croissants, danishes, and pastries are cooling on racks as you come in. Everything is made on-site in this low-key, homey place. Locals stop in for a coffee, a snack, and, of course, a sugar fix; some of them have just finished working out at the International YMCA across the street.

The baked goods are so reasonably priced here that you can hand over a fiver and still have change for the bus. For breakfast, the heavily packed strudel, heated up ever so slightly, is heavenly, as are the croissants oozing with custard. Greek pastries include kouranbiethes covered with powdered sugar, finikia cookies, and nut-filled melomakarona. The rum balls ($1.75) are dense and rich, and the florentines are a divine mix of chewy dried fruit half-dipped in chocolate. Entire cakes range from $8 to $15, depending on size.

To balance sweet with savoury, try the light and flaky spinach and cheese squares layered with golden filo dough. At a counter in the back of the shop, you'll find the fixings for a healthy lunch. The dozen salads on offer—bean, beet, potato, ratatouille, grilled veggie, fasolia—have a homemade quality and Greek inflections.

Hours: Mon.–Sat. 7:30 a.m.–8 p.m.; Sun. 8 a.m.–7 p.m.
Alcohol: No
Credit cards: No
Wheelchair access: Yes

5563 du Parc (@ St-Viateur)
(514) 279-7725
Metro: Place-des-Arts, 80 bus/Outremont, 160 bus

Pâtisserie de la Gare

Euro-style bakery with pastries, pasties, and potpies.

Located near the Montreal West train station, Pâtisserie de la Gare has a small-town atmosphere. Behind the lace curtains, pastries both savoury and sweet await those in search of a European-style afternoon treat.

At the counter, you'll find a row of unbearably cute marzipan figurines: frogs, lions, sheep, giraffes, panda bears, lobsters, ladybugs . . . Things get a little more serious on the next shelf down, which is stocked with all sorts of individual pastries (around $2.30 each). There are lots of two-tone specialties, like chocolate mousse with banana cream or pistachio cream, as well as éclairs, opera cakes, rum balls wrapped in marzipan, palmiers, fruit-studded scones, croissants, and custard tarts topped with all manner of glazed fruit. Homemade sorbets—passion fruit, orange, and Poire William—can be found in the freezer.

For a light lunch, sample some Old Country classics from the British Isles. There's one-person-size chicken pie, Scotch pie, steak and veggie pie, and quiches (all $2.50). The Cornish pasty is made of buttery, melt-in-your-mouth dough pinched together over a delicious filling of potatoes, meat, and carrots. The more modern California pie has a crust of sunflower seeds, oats, millet, and flax, and it's filled with a creamy vegetable mixture.

Hours: Mon.–Fri. 7 a.m.–7 p.m.; Sat. and Sun. 8 a.m.–7 p.m.
Alcohol: No
Credit cards: No; Interac accepted
Wheelchair access: Two steps

24 Westminster (@ Sherbrooke)
(514) 484-7565
Metro: Villa-Maria, 162 bus

Roberto Gelateria

Gourmet gelati fit for the gods.

Roberto is a great place for a date, especially if the object of your affections has a sweet tooth. The ice cream here is unlike anything you'll find elsewhere in the city, and the limited availability of Roberto's products only adds to their cachet.

The list of flavours has a distinctly Italian flair: Amaretto, tiramisu, zuppa inglese (English cream), pistachio, Baci (hazelnut and chocolate), Torrone (nougat), stacciatella alla mentha (mint with chocolate flakes), melone (cantaloupe). And there's also a refreshing granita, the lemon-scented sorbet that's served as a palate cleanser between courses of a big Italian meal. Staff are happy to let you do a taste test before choosing. Cups and cones are $2 to $3.95; mix two kinds for 50 cents more. Roberto's ice cream is instantly addictive, so you'll be relieved to know that you can buy it by the litre as well ($7).

This ice cream parlour is lovely to look at, with tall wooden tables and stools. It adjoins an equally appealing grocery store that stocks fine ingredients for home cooks and the necessities for a quick, inexpensive meal. Upstairs is a ristorante where affordable (about $10) gourmet pizzas, calzones, and focaccias can be enjoyed. Try the Pasta Roberto, a trio of tortellini with rosé sauce, fettuccine alfredo, and penne arrabbiata.

Hours: Tues. and Wed. 9 a.m.–11 p.m.;
Thurs.–Sat. 9 a.m.–midnight; Sun. 9 a.m.–11 p.m.
Alcohol: Yes
Credit cards: No; Interac accepted
Wheelchair access: No

2221 Bélanger (@ d'Iberville)
(514) 374-9844
Metro: d'Iberville

EATING
liquid
diet

Café Sinonet

Bubble tea bonanza!

Café Sinonet is a treasure trove of bubblicious beverages. It's one of the best places in town for bubble tea, a trendy drink made popular by Taiwanese teens at the end of the 1980s, which has since popped up on this side of the world. The bubbles are actually oversized tapioca pearls made of cassava root starch and caramel. They nestle at the bottom of your cup, and you suck them up through an extra-wide straw. The experience is not unlike drinking and chewing gum at the same time.

The drink menu here takes up two full pages. Some of the options under "foamed teas" include tropical punch, mint, peach, lemon, and the less-saccharine green tea. Another section lists creamy black or green tea with flavourings like wheat germ, red bean, egg yolk, sesame, and peanut. Then there's a variety of nontea drinks, such as mango, watermelon, pink lemonade, mint chocolate, and light and fruity pineapple. Taro, an Asian root vegetable, imparts a purple glow to the cup, and the mixture tastes a lot like melted bubble gum ice cream—pleasant but very, very sweet. Expect to pay $3 to $3.50 for this dessert-drink-sugar fix in an ambiance not unlike that of an after-school program, complete with Taiwanese alt-pop on the sound system.

Hours: Sun.–Thurs. noon–midnight; Fri. and Sat. noon–2 a.m.
Alcohol: No
Credit cards: No
Wheelchair access: No

71-A de la Gauchetière W. (@ Clark)
(514) 878-0572
Metro: Place-d'Armes

Cafétéria Las Palmas

Exotic shakes in a Colombian snackbar.

The walls of this small Colombian snackbar are covered with bright, colourful photos of just about every tropical fruit under the sun. The good-humoured owner will sometimes, school-teacher-style, use a stick to point out varieties you might not recognize by name. This will help you to make an informed decision about what flavour to order blended as a drink or frozen as a Popsicle. In addition to familiar essences like banana, papaya, strawberry, and mango, some of the more exotic options include lulo, tomate de arbol, guanabana, curuba, and mamey. Batidos—blenderized on the spot—sell for $2.75, with or without milk.

Las Palmas also serves excellent empanadas ($2). They have a thin, crispy corn-flour exterior and a seasoned beef interior, and they're served with a pungent green salsa. Other snacks include papa rellena ($4.50), a kind of mini shepherd's pie; chorizo sausage; and roast pork rind, called chicharrón. Although seating is limited to bar stools and a couple of tables, you can get a full meal here for $9, including arroz con pollo, a homey plate of chicken and rice.

An authentic community hangout, complete with Spanish TV, Las Palmas is a good place to heat up in winter or cool down with a licuado in summer.

Hours: Tues.–Sun. noon–9 p.m.
Alcohol: No
Credit cards: No
Wheelchair access: No

---

14 Rachel E. (@ St-Dominique)
(514) 987-1243
Metro: St-Laurent, 55 bus/Mont-Royal

Camellia Sinensis

An adventurous alternative to coffee culture.

This ethereal teahouse takes its name from the scientific word for the evergreen bush that yields tea leaves. Don't expect British-style high tea here—this hideaway is about reverence for tea traditions. Chinese tea comes in Yixing pots, mint tea comes in silver Moroccan vessels, and Japanese green tea comes in ceramic pots. Patrons mellow out at cozy tables around a gurgling fountain, sipping tea and nibbling on sweet snacks.

This popular salon de thé expanded a couple of years ago so that the boutique part of the business could have its own quarters. Silver tins of loose tea, stored on dark wood shelves, line the walls from floor to ceiling. Leaves are imported from points all over the world, including Africa, Indonesia, Thailand, Taiwan, India, China, and Japan. A few of the 50 varieties sold here are not distributed anywhere else in North American. Whether you opt for the black and smoky Russian Caravan or the rare Tung Ting, a wulong from Taiwan, helpful staff will inform you about the fine points of steeping.

Every Saturday at noon, the shop hosts a tasting event, allowing customers to compare 10 different blends that have been grouped according to country of origin, taste, or class (for groups of six, $7 each).

Hours: 11 a.m.–10 p.m. daily
Alcohol: No
Credit cards: Yes
Wheelchair access: Two steps

351 Emery (@ Sanguinet)
(514) 286-4002
Metro: Berri-UQAM

Cocktail Hawaii

Tremendously tropical drink and crêpe emporium.

Outside Cocktail Hawaii, two straw parasols blow bravely in the wind, as though they got lost on their way to a beach resort. The interior of this downtown oasis is just as incongruously tropical: salmon-pink walls, patio furniture, a fake parrot, and staff sporting Hawaiian shirts.

You can go on a blender bender here (for $2 to $5) by devising your own drinkable creation from a huge list of ingredients—strawberries, pineapple, almonds, guava, coconut milk, mango, and licorice, among others. One house specialty is the Kamikaze, a bright-green avocado shake that's satisfyingly thick, smooth, and filling. The Sahara is a mild and frothy combination of milk, honey, and banana. Alternately, dose yourself with vitamin C by downing some freshly squeezed orange juice.

Most of the solid-food selections on the menu ($4 to $7) are on the sweet side, including breakfast fare like malted crêpes and waffles. The Saint Marguerita crêpe is huge and heavy, spread with a generous dab of Nutella and filled with papaya, avocado, and banana. It's topped with chopped pistachios, honey, and achta, a fluffy white Lebanese cheese. The Mexicana crêpe contains apple and cinnamon, while the Sirène holds shrimp and crab in a white sauce. If you can bear to utter the word before noon, order the Tequila, and you'll be served an egg and maple syrup crêpe for $4.25.

Hours: Sun.–Thurs. 9 a.m.–1 a.m.; Fri. 9 a.m.–2 a.m.; Sat. 9 a.m.–4 a.m.
Alcohol: No
Credit cards: No
Wheelchair access: Yes

1645 de Maisonneuve (@ St-Mathieu)
(514) 933-8887
Metro: Guy-Concordia

Exos

International water cellar.

The people at Exos devote about as much attention to bottled water as sommeliers do to wine. This streamlined, three-storey space in the Quartier Latin is home to Montreal's one and only international water cellar. It houses a collection of brands from all over the world, each with its own distinctive taste and chemical properties.

After a visit here, you may never drink from the tap again. There are approximately 100 varieties on offer, from all sorts of sources and in all sorts of states: glacier water, spring water, carbonated water, iceberg water, distilled water, oxygenated water, and mineral water. Among them, you'll find Voss from Norway, which is bottled by Calvin Klein; Fiji, which is flavoured ever so faintly with coconut; Fiuggi from Italy; a collector's edition of Evian in a teardrop-shaped bottle; the Swedish Ramlösa; and Acqua Della Madonna in its distinctive blue container. The health bar also dispenses freshly squeezed juices, coffee, and tea—all made with spring water, of course!

Exos doesn't just have water on the brain. The second floor of this sleek white space is a design lab, where you'll find inventive furniture, like Philippe Starck stools made from garden gnomes, Swatch watches, and creations by local designers. The very top level is a health center. There you can have a massage, get a variety of beauty treatments, or relax on the terrace in warm weather.

Hours: 11 a.m.–9 p.m. daily
Alcohol: No
Credit cards: Yes
Wheelchair access: No

365 Emery (@ St-Denis)
(514) 842-3967
Metro: Berri-UQAM

Japanese Tea Garden

A sip of culture in a cup.

For a real taste of tea culture, there's nothing quite like a visit to the Japanese Pavilion at the Botanical Garden. There you'll find the tea garden, unveiled in the fall of 2002. It's a memorable setting in which to appreciate the importance of tea in Japan. Like the traditional tea garden, known as roji, it's divided into outer and inner spaces that lead to the bamboo-accented chashitsu, or teahouse.

As you move through these spaces, you're supposed to leave the worries of the world behind. The overall design is organic, but each component—stepping stones, fountain, moss, plants—is carefully chosen to invoke serenity and facilitate communion with the natural world.

Green-tea tastings ($2) are held several days a week in the early afternoon. Every Saturday, the full 45-minute Cha-No-Yu tea ceremony ($6 for participants, and $3 for spectators) is performed by the Urasenke School of Montreal. The school is dedicated to fostering this aspect of Japanese culture. Each movement is strictly predetermined, yet the performance as a whole creates a sense of tranquility and timelessness.

While you're there, if you have the urge to commune even more closely with nature, pop over to the adjacent Insectarium. Since 1993, its visitors have been offered unique snacks: chocolate-covered grasshoppers, ant cakes, tamari-fried stick insects, and spicy locusts.

Hours: May 3 through November 3, roughly 9 a.m.–7 p.m. daily
Alcohol: No
Credit cards: No
Wheelchair access: Yes

4101 Sherbrooke E. (in the Jardin botanique de Montréal)
(514) 872-0607
Metro: Pie IX or Viau

Salon de Thé O-Cha-I
Tea and tea-based desserts.

From O-Cha-I's basement windows, you can peer out at the snow-drifts along St-Denis and warm your hands on a piping hot pot of tea. This place is a welcome retreat for those who miss the teahouses that have closed on the strip over the years. Despite the subterranean setting, or maybe thanks to it, the atmosphere is cozy—it's definitely a spot where you can feel at home unwinding by yourself.

The very attentive family that runs the place sells and serves more than 50 varieties of tea—green, black, and even white. There are teas from India, Africa, Japan, and China, as well as a bubblegum tisane for kids. You can peruse O-Cha-I's stock of tea-related gifts or check out the watercolours by local artists that line the brick walls.

In addition to a few Asian snacks, there are also decent desserts, some of which are made with tea. Recommended are the Earl Grey cookies; the green tea cake ($2.95), which is moist, spongy, and not too sweet; the doughy bon-bons stuffed with dark chocolate; and the lemon and poppy seed cheesecake ($3.50). Take a look at the list of intriguing ice creams, which come in all sorts of fun flavours—like ginger, litchi, red bean, sesame, green tea, jasmine, and chai, that delectable spicy-sweet Indian beverage of hot milk, sugar, cardamom, and cinnamon.

Hours: Mon.–Wed. noon–11 p.m.; Thurs.–Sun. noon–midnight
Alcohol: No
Credit cards: Visa; Interac accepted
Wheelchair access: No

4517 St-Denis (@ Mont-Royal)
(514) 982-9229
Metro: Mont-Royal

DRINKING
with food

La Cabane de Portugal

When you just can't decide where to meet up with friends, La Cabane is a great fallback place. There's nothing über-trendy about it, but that's part of its appeal. It's got big windows looking out at the Main, it plays eighties hits (good, bad, and just plain ugly), and the waitresses keep the pitchers coming. For lunch or a late-night meal, there's affordable Portuguese fare, like grilled pork (bifana) or chicken breast sandwiches ($8.95), served on big crusty rolls. The daily specials are often surprisingly good for the price ($7 to $13). The list features a range of meat, pasta, and seafood dishes—Matane shrimp, grilled fish, pepper steak. Depending on your mood, La Cabane can feel a bit more like a restaurant or a bit more like a bar.

Hours: 11:30 a.m.–3 a.m. daily

3872 St-Laurent (@ St-Cuthbert)
(514) 843-7283
Metro: St-Laurent, 55 bus

Café Sarajevo

This Bosnian hideaway has an otherworldly atmosphere. It's somewhere between a lounge and a coffeehouse, with its stone walls and its ad-hoc arrangement of couches and tables set on red carpets. Live musicians and belly dancers help transport you to another time and place. Sarajevo is a cozy spot to enjoy a glass of wine and taste the cuisine of the former Yugoslavia. The bartender does the cooking between drink orders. In addition to cheese or meat plates ($8), there's cevapi, salty beef and lamb sausages that contrast nicely with ajwar, a spicy and sweet sauce made with roasted red peppers. The flavourful marinated chicken is served with rice and salad topped with olives, nuts, and raisins. A mixed plate for two is $28.

Hours: Tues. and Wed. 8 p.m.–12:30 a.m.;
Thurs. 5 p.m.–1:30 a.m.; Fri. and Sat. 5 p.m.–3 a.m.

2080 Clark (@ Ontario)
(514) 284-5629
Metro: St-Laurent

Casa del Popolo

This small storefront is the low-key unofficial headquarters of the city's counterculture scene. It hosts a wide spectrum of events: spoken word, book launches, comic jams, film screenings, and live music from folk to punk rock to atmospheric soundscapes. Although the place is often standing-room-only at night, you can sit down and munch before dark. The menu is vegetarian from head to toe, and it mainly features healthy soups, salads, and sandwiches ($4.59 each, or $9 for all three). Wash down your meal with a pint of one of the local beers on tap. Typical ingredients here are veggie pâté, artichokes, tomatoes, grilled red peppers, pesto mayonnaise, dijon mustard, Bocconcini, and tofu. While eating, check out the list of upcoming events marked on a large chalkboard on the wall.

Hours: noon–3 a.m. daily

4873 St-Laurent (@ St-Joseph)
(514) 284-3804
Metro: Laurier, 51 bus/St-Laurent, 55 bus

Laïka

With its giant leg-level windows, Laïka works the fishbowl effect with great success. The décor, with its ultra-designed blocks of muted colour, is a hip and soothing backdrop for breakfast, lunch, dinner, or just a cocktail—like vodka and Red Bull. Morning fare includes a first-rate café au lait and several frittatas made with delicious combos: pear, endive, blue cheese, and walnuts; or apple, curry, Brie, and pine nuts. As night falls, the DJ booth gets busy, and the coffee crowd is slowly replaced by the alcohol-minded. To go with drinks, the menu offers excellent alternatives to the basic chicken wing. There are snacks in the form of quesadillas with black beans and coriander, and panini ($6.50) layered with yummy fillings—try sausage, chèvre, onion, and zuc-chini; or prosciutto and Provolone.

Hours: Mon.–Fri. 8:30 a.m.–3 a.m.;
Sat. and Sun. 9 a.m.–3 a.m.

4040 St-Laurent (@ Duluth)
(514) 842-8088
Metro: St-Laurent, 55 bus/Mont-Royal, 97 bus

McKibbins Irish Pub

McKibbins occupies three storeys of an old downtown walkup. The cellar is an intimate room with dartboards and dark corners, the third floor is for dancing, and the middle floor is for high-spirited music and meals. The menu is a cornucopia of Celtic classics. There's the Cork chips and curry ($4.75)—big, thick fries with lots of mildly spicy sauce served on the side. Fish in a beer batter and chips come with peas and tartar sauce. Other options include Irish stew made with lamb and potatoes, steak and kidney pie, and chicken and leek pie ($10.45). For the fainter of heart, there's a grilled veggie sandwich served with mashed potatoes. McKibbins presents live music on an almost nightly basis and stocks a good selection of draft beers and scotches—with an Irish bias, of course.

Hours: 11 a.m.–3 a.m. daily

1426 Bishop (@ de Maisonneuve W.)
(514) 288-1580
Metro: Guy-Concordia

Le Va et Vient

Le Va et Vient bills itself as a "cultural bistro," and it certainly plays a key role in the St-Henri scene. Music shows take place on its stage on a regular basis, its walls are dedicated to exhibiting art, and its tables are full of neighbourhood types who feel equally comfortable reading alone or socializing over a drink. The menu makes stops around the globe. A bowl of rib-tickling chili ($7.25) comes con or non carne; both the vegetarian and chicken versions go superbly with the microbrews on offer. There are also lots of meal-size salads, pastas, burgers, and quesadillas. Some of the snacks are fun too, including warm cheese, chorizo, olives, breads, and spreads.

Hours: Mon.–Wed. 11 a.m.–10 p.m.;
Thurs. and Fri. 11 a.m.–11 p.m.; Sat. 10:30 a.m.–11 p.m.;
Sun. 10 a.m.–3 p.m.

3706 Notre Dame W. (@ Bourget)
(514) 940-2330
Metro: St-Henri or Lionel-Groulx

DRINKING
home
brew

L'Amère à Boire

A rustic brewpub with an Eastern European bent, L'Amère à Boire attracts connoisseurs. The beer menu makes for interesting reading, as it details the origins of the pub's 14 products. The lagers and ales are brewed on the premises using traditional recipes; genuine hops and pure barley malt go into the mix. Pilsner fans should sample Cerná Horá, made with yeast imported from the Czech Republic—it's so authentic that L'Amère supplies it to Montreal's Czech consulate. To every beer, there's also a season: in winter, spicy Christmas ale is brewed; there's German-style Oktoberfest beer in the fall; and when spring arrives, it's time for the full-bodied Bière du Mars. The top floor of this pub is occupied by a restaurant called L'Hospoda (Czech for "bistro"), which serves beer-inspired fare.

Hours: 2 p.m.–3 a.m. daily

2049 St-Denis (@ Sherbrooke)
(514) 282-7448
Metro: Berri-UQAM or Sherbrooke

Brutopia

There's a dearth of craft breweries in the downtown area, but Brutopia picks up the slack. This cozy space is modelled on the typical British drinking establishment, and it specializes in English-style ales. India pale ale (IPA), an amber beer with a strong malt flavour and a hopped finish, is popular here. Brutopia always has the following selections on tap: extra-blonde, raspberry blonde, nut brown ale, and honey beer (combine the last two for a honey brown). Often, there are also a couple of more unusual concoctions to sample, like American wheat, smoked porter, or rye brews. With its live music, friendly staff, board games, full kitchen with a decent menu, and two terraces, this cheerful, low-key pub provides its customers with a number of good ways to amuse themselves.

Hours: Mon.–Thurs., Sat. and Sun. 3 p.m.–3 a.m.;
Fri. noon–3 a.m.

1219 Crescent (@ Ste-Catherine)
(514) 393-9277
Metro: Peel

Cheval Blanc

Cheval Blanc became the Montreal originator of the microbrewery trend in the late 1980s, when it obtained the city's first brewpub licence. Its ambiance, though, seems to derive from an even earlier era. The sleek chrome and formica décor, accented with red lanterns and original art works, recalls a 1930s film noir set. There are usually five kinds of brew on offer in this atmospheric tavern: pale, red, a white Belgian-style wheat beer, amber, and a black made with Belgian yeast. And look out for the flavour of the month, which might be cranberry, strawberry, or maple. The bar also serves a brand put out by the label that shares its name: Coup de Grisou, a musky, full-bodied buckwheat ale.

Hours: Wed.–Sat. 3 p.m.–3 a.m.; Sun.–Tues. 3 p.m.–1 a.m.

809 Ontario E. (@ St-Hubert)
(514) 522-0211
Metro: Berri-UQAM

Dieu du Ciel

You'll find Dieu du Ciel on a residential Plateau street corner, its brewing vats gleaming appealingly through the window. The inside of this popular neighbourhood pub is dark, smoky, and loud. One of the stars of the beer list, which is full of whimsical names, is an unusual smoked ale called La Charbonnière ("coal vendor"). It's made with smoked malt, which gives it a complex and distinctive taste. Fumisterie is a hemp beer with nutty accents, Nativité Blonde is a German wheat beer with a hint of banana, and the Déesse Nocturne is a stout with a foamy head and an aroma of chocolate. A 4-ounce tasting cup is $1, and there are jumbo pitchers, called "giraffes," that contain 120 ounces of brew. Some offerings are more than seven percent alcohol, so order a snack to soak it up.

Hours: 3 p.m.–3 a.m. daily

---

29 Laurier W. (@ Clark)
(514) 490-9555
Metro: Laurier, 51 bus

Le Sergent-Recruteur

This two-floor business is named for the recruiting sergeants of centuries past, whose job it was to make the rounds of taverns in search of sailors who had wandered away from their ships to go swimming in drink. A pint of bitter is hand-pumped here, just like real British ale. It has an almost savoury taste and not much fizz. Other brews on tap include a light and tasty wheat ale called Nuit Blanche, along with a honey blonde and a watermelon blonde. Finger foods are available. On weekends, live music gets things hopping—there's rock, funk, jazz, and pretty much everything in between. Le Sergent also hosts weekly storytelling soirées in the francophone tradition.

Hours: Sun.–Wed. 5 p.m.–3 a.m.; Thurs.–Sat. 4 p.m.–3 a.m.

4650 St-Laurent (@ Villeneuve)
(514) 287-1412
Metro: Laurier or Mont-Royal

Réservoir

Fans of homemade hooch should reserve some time for Réservoir, a new Plateau hotspot. Its on-site facilities produce finely tuned brews, from sweet Scotch ale to a pungent wheat-based amber. The slightly spicy Bière de Mars is spruced up with cranberries, while the Weizen, a white beer, is a pleasantly perfumed surprise. The space itself is classy and cozy, with subdued lighting that makes you look tanned at any time of the year—almost. Part bar, part resto, Réservoir also sets out to answer the question of what goes best with beer—besides more beer, of course. Delectable draughts are paired with a selection of finger foods that will have you pitching out your pretzels. The black bean chili with chipotle peppers, fried calamari, and hummus are healthy complements to a night of taste testing.

Hours: Tues. noon–2 a.m.; Wed.–Fri. noon–3 a.m.;
Sat. 3 p.m.–3 a.m.; Sun. 3 p.m.–2 a.m.

9 Duluth E. (@ St-Laurent)
(514) 849-7779
Metro: Mont-Royal or St-Laurent, 55 bus

DRINKING
in a
pint

Barouf

To really taste the city French-style, you have to visit Barouf. In terms of design and atmosphere, it's one of the most charming bars on the St-Denis strip. It so fully encapsulates the best of francophone Montreal that it's conceivable that one of these days busloads of tourists will stop here to see how the other half lives. Round mirrors transform the room into an Impressionist painting, while the wood panelling, quirky statuettes, and rotary-dial phone lend it a timeless feel. There's a great selection of beers, from Belgian and British imports to the latest from the Quebec microbreweries—like Boréal, Cheval Blanc, and Belle Gueule—plus a good lineup of scotches. During World Cup season, it's the unofficial headquarters for French soccer fans. For some off-season action, try the foosball table in the back.

Hours: 1:30 p.m.–3 a.m. daily

4171 St-Denis (@ Rachel)
(514) 844-0119
Metro: Mont-Royal

Bily Kun

From the moment it opened, Bily Kun has had one of the hottest cinq-à-sept sessions in town. In this long, narrow space, the classic brasserie ambiance is enlivened with a few funky twists, including several mounted ostrich heads that peer curiously at customers. The name Bily Kun means "white horse" in Czech (as in Cheval Blanc, a topnotch local brewery whose products are sold here). Upstairs is an art and performance venue called O Patro Vys (also a Czech name), which opened in the fall of 2002. In keeping with the owners' affinity for Eastern Europe, the bar is stocked with absinthe from the Czech Republic. This legendary green liquor, banned outright for almost a century, is a potent concoction made of wormwood. Absinthe drinkers engage in a certain ritual involving a spoon, sugar, and a match—visit Bily Kun and see for yourself.

Hours: 3 p.m.–3 a.m. daily

---

354 Mont-Royal E. (@ St-Denis)
(514) 845-5392
Metro: Mont-Royal

Blizzarts

Many Montrealers consider Blizzarts to be pretty close to the perfect bar. What's cool about this is that they like it for different reasons. Part lounge, part dance club, Blizzarts manages to draw a relaxed, diverse crowd, from skaters to electro-intellectos to B-boys and girls. Part of the attraction is the bar's excellent roster of DJs who specialize in the rare sounds of drum and bass, funk, reggae, hip-hop, and breaks. The dance floor is fairly small, but some nights it sees a lot of booty-shaking. There's also an assortment of kitschy furniture to plunk down on when you're tired out from busting moves. Lounge chairs can be arranged to seat intimate groups. Blizzarts also has art exhibits on its walls.

Hours: 7 p.m.–3 a.m. daily

3956A St-Laurent (@ Bagg)
(514) 843-4860
Metro: St-Laurent, 55 bus

Old Dublin

Montreal's Irish community has deep roots, and so does the Old Dublin. On St. Patrick's Day, needless to say, this place is absolutely nuts—but a watered-down version of that joie de vivre can be found here on just about any other night. Look for the little green building tucked behind a big parking lot on a downtown side street. One of the most enduring traditional pubs of its kind, Old Dublin has nary a newfangled angle. In this cozy space, listening to the banter of the regulars, you'll be distracted from whatever stresses you are seeking to escape. Traditional Irish musicians perform here regularly, and the kitchen serves up traditional Irish grub for lunch and dinner.

Hours: Mon.–Sat. noon–3 a.m.; Sun. 2 p.m.–3 a.m.

1219A University (@ René-Lévesque)
(514) 861-4448
Metro: Bonaventure

Quartier Latin Pub

Somehow, Quartier Latin manages to be both hip and plush but not at all pretentious. It's designed for maximum style and comfort, with two separate seating areas and a patio that faces the street. As soon as you're seated, your server will bring peanuts and pretzels for you to munch on as you delve into the list of cocktails, microbrewery products, and pints of imported brands from the U.K. and Europe, like Harp, Guinness, and Stella Artois. If you want to avoid the hoi polloi, retreat to the room at the back and play some billiards. If you want to be entertained, take in the live DJs and bands that deliver jazzy funk, hip-hop, and electronica. The general atmosphere is somewhere between those of a British pub and a trendy lounge, and Quartier Latin succeeds on both counts.

Hours: 3 p.m.–3 a.m. daily

318 Ontario E. (@ St-Denis)
(514) 845-3301
Metro: Berri-UQAM

Yer Mad

This subterranean pub, inspired by the kind of drinking establishment you might find in Brittany, a region of France, is popular with the francophone university crowd. But it's also a great little hideaway for people who live in the area and want a break from the pulsating beat of the Gay Village. Yer Mad occupies a rustic space; its walls are panelled with wood and it's furnished with wooden benches. In addition to a selection of imported beers, the bar offers ciders from far away and from the rural areas surrounding Montreal. Try one mixed with Guinness or white beer. Or you may have a hankering for a glass of hydromel—Yer Mad also serves mead, wine made from honey that has roots among the ancient Druids. And there's a foosball table, on which intense "baby-foot" tournaments take place.

Hours: Mon.–Fri. 2 p.m.–3 a.m.; Sat. and Sun. 4 p.m.–3 a.m.

---

901 Maisonneuve E. (@ St-Christophe)
(514) 522-9392
Metro: Berri-UQAM

DRINKING straight

L'Hypertaverne Edgar

When it was launched by the owners of the funky Diable Vert on St-Denis, this hypertaverne was an instant success with the after-work crowd and neighbourhood yuppies. The eye-catching décor makes effective use of wood strips, cylindrical lamps, and cushioned banquettes. Handpicked brews from Belle Gueule, Cheval Blanc, Griffon, McAuslan, and St-Amboise are on tap, and there's a good range of imported bottles, like Leffe, Foster's, Tuborg, Bass, and Dos Equis. But the real stars here are the half-dozen thoughtfully selected wines available by the glass. For a white, try the fumée blanc; if you're in a red mood, order a glass of Château de Parenchère. A cheese selection—blue, Brie, Gouda, Gruyère, and the Quebec-made Victor and Berthold—is offered for sharing; the self-absorbed can order cheese in individual portions. If you're feeling meat-minded, you can get a Euro-dog.

Hours: Wed.–Sun. 3 p.m.–3 a.m.

1562 Mont-Royal E. (@ Fabre)
(514) 521-4661
Metro: Mont-Royal

L'Île Noire

L'Île Noire is an authentic Scottish pub located in what has long been the francophone heart of the city. The setting is warm and cozy, with its wood accents, cream tones, and smattering of tartan. The place is exclusive enough to appeal to a well-heeled professional crowd, but it's laid-back enough to provide a comfortable environment for almost anyone. More than 100 types of whisky are served at L'Île Noire, most of them single malt. Both the curious amateur and the connoisseur will find the selection dizzying. Those in the know with dough might want to fork over $500 for a dram of Macallan circa 1946 or sample the Auchentoshan '65, but far more affordable options are available. There are also English beers on tap, including the hard-to-find Younger's Tartan from Scotland.

Hours: 3 p.m.–3 a.m. daily

342 Ontario E. (@ St-Denis)
(514) 982-0866
Metro: Berri-UQAM

Modavie

This is an upscale but not too polished place for sitting, smoking, and sipping. There's a good selection of wines: more than 200 varieties are stocked in the glass-front wine cellar, including ice wines and many New World wines; about 10 are available by the glass. Then there are the spirits: choose from among several brands of cognac, scotch, eau-de-vie, and port. Modavie offers a line of flambéed coffees, including a house creation made with Amaretto, Galiano, and Frangelico (the same triple threat is available with blueberry tea). Snazzy jazz snakes through the space—most nights, live bands perform. Appetizers and fine cheeses are served, but if you've really got a case of the munchies, there is a restaurant upstairs, albeit a rather pricey one.

Hours: Sun.–Thurs. 11 a.m.–11 p.m.;
Fri. and Sat. 11 a.m.–midnight

---

1 St-Paul W. (@ St-Laurent)
(514) 287-9582
Metro: Place-d'Armes

Sofa

Like the piece of furniture it's named for, Sofa is a good spot to unwind after a hard day's work. The ambiance at this porto bar is swank, suave, and spirited. In summer, its large windows, within squinting distance of St-Denis, are thrown open. In the early evenings, Sofa is all about sitting and sipping your drink. The house specialty is port, sold by the glass, and there's a good array to choose from: white ports, 10-year-old tawny ports, and 20-year-old vintages. In summer, Sofa mixes up an excellent sangria porto. Jameson Irish whisky, Glenlivet, and Chivas Regal are available. Seven days a week, there are DJs on duty, and on Wednesday through Saturday nights live bands perform soul, funk, and jazz.

Hours: 4 p.m.–3 a.m. daily

---

451 Rachel E. (@ Rivard)
(514) 285-1011
Metro: Mont-Royal

Upstairs

Despite its name, Upstairs is downstairs. Patrons gather here to enjoy a mellow blend of live jazz, spirits, and sustenance. The large wooden bar dispenses a well-considered selection of straight or mixed drinks, including numerous brands of scotch, port, cognac, and champagne. Red and white wines are sold by the glass, with or without a meal from the haute but homey on-site restaurant. Upstairs has long been a prime destination for jazz lovers, and its small stage, complete with piano, accommodates a parade of local and visiting performers. And because the space is small, most audience members feel like they have front-row seats. The microscopic terrace is the setting for chess matches during warm months; in cold weather, the inside space exudes an irresistible coziness.

Hours: Mon.–Thurs. noon–1 a.m.; Fri. noon–3 a.m.; Sat. 5 p.m.–3 a.m.; Sun. 5 p.m.–1 a.m.

1254 Mackay (@ Ste-Catherine)
(514) 931-6808
Metro: Guy-Concordia

Whisky Café

Single malts are the specialty at the sophisticated Whisky Café, located in Mile End, north of the nightlife district. In addition to a considerable selection of port wines, grappas, cognacs, and calvados, there's a list of over 100 whiskies—hailing from Scotland, Ireland, and the Americas—for you to mull over. This is a good place to blow your budget on a tasting menu that pairs drinks with delicacies like beluga caviar, Belgian chocolates, cheeses, or smoked trout. Slickly designed and outfitted with booths and bistro tables, Whisky attracts a well-heeled crowd of 25-plussers. Some of them come to visit the cigar lounge, a separate, ventilated area with leather armchairs and a humidor of Cohibas and Monte Cristos. The bathrooms are something to behold—check out the only female urinal in the city.

Hours: Mon.–Fri. 5 p.m.–3 a.m.; Sat. 6 p.m.–3 a.m.; Sun. 7:30 p.m.–3 a.m.

5800 St-Laurent (@ Bernard)
(514) 278-2646
Metro: St-Laurent, 55 bus

DRINKING cocktails

Cabaret Mado

The brainchild of Montreal's most famous drag queen, Mado, this establishment upholds the transvestite tradition in the heart of the Gay Village. Decorated in the style of a 1920s cabaret, the space features red-velvet drapes and baroque touches. Theatricality is the order of the day here, and everything is done with a good dose of humour. The club welcomes a straight and queer clientele to partake of its nightly activities. Mado herself performs weekly, occasionally hosting the bingo soirées that have brought her fame over the last decade. Portraits of Mado in outrageous outfits are displayed throughout the bar. There are daily happy hours and theme evenings—like drag karaoke night, or Star Search night—followed by dancing for all. What you'll find here is a celebration of quirkiness and the best of kétaine culture.

Hours: 4 p.m.–3 a.m. daily

1115 Ste-Catherine E. (@ Beaudry)
(514) 525-7566
Metro: Beaudry

Jello Bar

Things were shagadelic at Jello Bar long before Austin Powers made his groovy entrance. Since it opened, in 1995, it's won fans among the local cocktail culture and cultivated a list of famous patrons—from Nicolas Cage to Bette Midler. Its décor certainly has some of the kitschiest touches in town—the eclectic mix of lamps, armchairs, and rounded edges is designed to take you back to the early sixties. The music, however, takes you all over the world. There's live and spun R&B, funk, swing, jazz, and salsa. Those interested in a dance lesson can usually pick one up on the dance floor. The house specialty is martinis, and Jello Bar offers a rainbow of more than 50 variations, in addition to the classic James Bond version. Blue Lagoon, for instance, gets its colour from Blue Curaçao, which is added to vodka and pineapple juice.

Hours: Tues.–Fri. 5 p.m.–3 a.m.; Sat. 9 p.m.–3 a.m.

151 Ontario E. (@ de Bullion)
(514) 285-2621
Metro: St-Laurent

737

Look up, look way up . . . to the top of Place Ville-Marie, one of Montreal's tallest skyscrapers. Perched 40 stories above the city, 737 is worth a visit for its stunning 360-degree views. This multi-level space houses a bar, a discotheque, and an upscale restaurant. The cinq-à-sept is popular with people who work in nearby offices—they ride the elevator to unwind with cocktails, especially on Thursdays. On weekends, the sound system starts thumping out dance music, attracting a party crowd. This is a great place for people-watching over a high-flying drink, especially during the summer, when the action spills outside onto two terraces on the east and west sides of the building. Not recommended for those who are afraid of heights.

Hours: bar, Wed.–Fri. 4:30 p.m.–10 p.m.; disco, Fri. and Sat. 10:30 p.m.–3 a.m.

---

1 Place Ville-Marie, level PH2 (University @ Cathcart)
(514) 397-0737
Metro: Bonaventure

Sir Winston Churchill Pub

The Sir Winston Churchill has long epitomized Montreal's downtown anglo scene. When it opened, in 1967, one of the city's most glorious years, it was the first bar on the Crescent strip. These days, it's a three-level affair: the pub is on the lower level; a cigar lounge, affectionately known as Winnie's, occupies the next floor up; and the top storey is home to a classy club called Karina's. The pub's interior is dark, wood-panelled, and cozy. The kitchen produces a mixture of Cajun dishes and British pub fare. During the two-for-one happy hour, this is a good place to come for chitchat with friends. Upstairs, you can dance until the wee hours. The venue attracts business types, university students, tourists, and talkers—including some of the city's best-known journalists.

Hours: 11 a.m.–3 a.m. daily

1455 Crescent (@ de Maisonneuve)
(514) 288-3814
Metro: Peel

Le Swimming

Le Swimming packs in a lot of entertainment options under one roof. At the back of this large bar you'll find about a dozen pool tables (free before 5 p.m.; there's an hourly charge after that). If it's just talk you're after, take a table near the windows, which are left open in summer to create a sort of indoor terrace. The bar's second-floor location allows for excellent people-watching— you get a unique perspective on the bald spots and cleavage passing below. DJs spin tunes midweek, but most nights Le Swimming is also a hopping live venue, so there's often a cover charge. A stage near the front is used by a diverse collection of local bands performing funk, retro covers, ska, swing, folk, and rock. There's a decent-sized dance floor if the music sways you.

Hours: noon–3 a.m. daily

3643 St-Laurent (@ Prince-Arthur)
(514) 282-7665
Metro: Sherbrooke or St-Laurent, 55 bus

Typhoon Lounge

A bar to call its own was the one thing N.D.G.'s commercial strip needed to complete its much-heralded 1990s renaissance. And Typhoon was it. The bar has a mainstream party atmosphere that attracts groups of younger area residents, as well as the occasional couple seeking a place to have a quiet conversation. Martinis are the specialty of the house, and Typhoon plays all sorts of inventive variations on the theme. Suede, for instance, is made of vodka, espresso, and Frangelico, a hazelnut-perfumed liqueur. There are also the Martini Ting, made with grapefruit juice; the Summer, with Southern Comfort, Amaretto, watermelon liqueur, and cranberry juice; and the Typhoon, created with vodka, melon liqueur, Blue Curaçao, 7-Up, lime, and grenadine. Steady yourself with something from the menu, which includes a whopping list of burgers.

Hours: Mon.–Wed. 4 p.m.–3 a.m.; Thurs.–Sun. noon–3 a.m.

5752 Monkland (@ Wilson)
(514) 482-4448
Metro: Villa-Maria

DRINKING
on the cheap

Bar Normand

This place is strictly for nostalgia fans. Nothing about it is here, now, or happening—it's pregentrification. It's the kind of bar where disgruntled old men cry into their beer. Perhaps they're crying for yesteryear, a time when brasseries like this one would never dream of putting up "Bienvenue aux Dames" and "Verres Stérilisées" signs. It has a fantastic chrome and tile exterior and in its heavy door is a porthole window. Inside, the mosaic work continues with a ceramic study of Maurice "The Rocket" Richard. The mural, depicting the hockey player in his high-flying glory, adorns the wall behind the bar. Beer here is extremely cheap; so is use of the pool table at the back. On good nights, the place exudes a joie de vivre, but on bad nights being there is like sitting in an empty swimming pool. Try to liven up the atmosphere by making a few selections from the jukebox—if it's working.

Hours: 9 a.m.–midnight daily

1550 Mont-Royal E. (@ Fabre)
(514) 525-8748
Metro: Mont-Royal

Barfly

Barfly is the definition of hole-in-the-wall, and that's just what it aims to be. Its unremarkable exterior is punctuated by an equally nondescript door. Climb a few rickety stairs, step inside, and you'll come face to face with a single pool table—it practically overwhelms the small, sombre room it inhabits. If you like dark corners, this is your place, but you'll often find that most of the stools have been claimed by a slew of regulars who come here to partake of the inexpensive liquor and shoot the breeze. Conversation at Barfly is usually good fun. Several times a week, the bar presents a remarkable range of live music on its tiny stage. Bands playing everything from punk rock to folksy folk show up here, and Sunday's bluegrass jams will get your toes tapping.

Hours: 4 p.m.–3 a.m. daily

4062-A St-Laurent (@ Duluth)
(514) 993-5154
Metro: St-Laurent, 55 bus

Bifteck

Bifteck is the alternative scene's answer to Cheers: hang out here long enough, and everybody knows your name. Staff members and patrons have intricate ties to the local music scene, so you'll often hear bits of conversation like, "No, their first album was the best." After playing at nearby venues, music celebs large and small have been known to drop by Biftek for a nightcap. The barmaids are legends in their own right—some achieve the status of local sex symbol while others go on to greater glory. On the weekends, when the bar gets busy, management opens the second floor to add more seats and pool tables to the basic watering hole setup. Biftek stays crowded until closing, when staff members shout hollow threats to get people to finish their beer.

Hours: 2 p.m.–3 a.m. daily

3702 St-Laurent (@ Guilbault)
(514) 844-6211
Metro: Sherbrooke or St-Laurent, 55 bus

Cock'n Bull

A traditional pub situated a little west of most of the action, Cock'n Bull attracts a mixture of students and locals. Behind the bright-red door, the atmosphere strikes a pleasant balance between British pub and Québécois tavern. Outside, there's a teeny-tiny terrace; inside, dartboards share wall space with stained glass panels. Incidentally, a cock'n bull is a tall tale, and over the years a lot of yarns have been spun here, fuelled by pints of Guinness and pitchers of domestic beer. On a regular basis, a crew of musicians will turn up, plug in their equipment a few feet from your face, and start playing blues or danceable rock. At one time, the pub's kitchen served Chinese food, which, in addition to filling you up, made you conveniently thirstier, but it closed in 2002 and has yet to be replaced.

Hours: noon–3 a.m. daily

1944 Ste-Catherine W. (@ Fort)
(514) 933-4556
Metro: Atwater

Pasalymani

Not everyone likes this place, but those who do feel right at home here—literally. Pasalymani is like someone's apartment. The older waitress who used to add to the effect by shuffling around in her slippers has been replaced by younger, hipper personalities. Despite the name, you don't have to "pass all ya money" to drink here. Beer is very cheap; quarts are an especially good bargain. The jukebox in the back has some fun tunes, including a few Johnny Cash classics, and there's a tiny stage where live bands play. Located in a row of forgettable Greek establishments, what was once just a hardcore drinking room for AA dropouts has become an alternative venue in bar-strapped Mile End. But expect absolutely no frills of any kind here.

Hours: 2 p.m.–3 a.m. daily

5845 du Parc (@ Bernard)
(514) 277-8936
Metro: Place-des-Arts, 80 bus

Wheel Club

It's definitely off the beaten track, but that's part of the Wheel Club's charm. The music here is the antithesis of electronica—deep country, jive, and bluegrass beats from the backwoods. The club's weekly Hillbilly Night has been going strong for more than 30 years, and it attracts musicians from all over. Dance themes and cheap drinks get both the old-timers and the young 'uns moving. The atmosphere feels kind of like that of a rec room in the home of someone with really laid-back parents. There's wood panelling on the walls, and the furniture has seen better days. And, of course, there are darts—in fact, the Wheel Club is home to several dart leagues. This place is a great alternative to the downtown or Plateau scenes, so put on your dancing shoes and head west.

Hours: Mon.–Thurs. noon–midnight;
Fri. and Sat. noon–2 a.m.

3373 Cavendish (@ Sherbrooke)
(514) 489-3322
Metro: Vendôme, 105 bus

DRINKING with fresh air

Complexe Bourbon

This sprawling, blocklong building, which houses restaurants, bars, and a hotel, is a cornerstone of Montreal's thriving Gay Village. You may find the maze of rooms and staircases initially daunting, but you're bound to find a spot where you feel comfortable. In summer, decisions about where to sit are made even more difficult by the multitude of sun-drenched open-air terraces. Crack open a Corona and choose between the ground-floor patio, the rear deck surrounded by greenery, or the top level overlooking the street. Delve deeper and investigate the on-site disco, Club Backtrack, which turns back the hands of time on weekends by playing hits from the last 30 years. On other nights, hard house, trance, and tribal get a mixed crowd grooving. Zone, a men-only bar, also shares the building.

Hours: 24/7, except the club

1474 Ste-Catherine E. (@ Alexandre-de-Sève)
(514) 529-6969
Metro: Papineau or Beaudry

Foufounes Électriques

For years—since the early 1980s, in fact—Foufounes has been a must-stop on the alternative circuit. Dedicated to showcasing raw talent before it hits the mainstream, the club boasts a stellar list of acts. Here are just a few of the notables who have graced the Foufounes stage: Nirvana, Mano Negra, William Burroughs, and Marianne Faithfull; local celebs include Dubmatique, Jean Leloup, and the Pag. A meeting place for all forms of underground culture, the club hosts a range of events, including concerts, barbecues, art shows, and sideshows. On the second-floor deck, you can soak up the ambiance from the outside—it's kind of like a very urban back yard. Foufounes is a home away from home for fans of goth, hardcore, emo, new wave, ska, industrial, reggae, and rock—and they all get along here. Living proof that anarchy and alcohol do mix.

Hours: 3 p.m.–3 a.m. daily

87 Ste-Catherine E. (@ de Bullion)
(514) 844-5539
Metro: Berri-UQAM or St-Laurent

Jardin Nelson

Jardin Nelson isn't just a bistro with a terrace—it's pretty much all terrace. In this multilevel courtyard, customers are protected from the elements by huge canvas umbrellas, and on cool evenings, space heaters keep their toes toasty. Surrounded by trees and flowers, and illuminated by artistic lighting, the bistro itself occupies an 1812 house. At noon each day, classical musicians command the al fresco stage, and jazz performers take over on weekend afternoons. Located just off Place Jacques-Cartier, a square teeming with street performers, Jardin Nelson is popular with tourists, but it's also a change-of-season indicator for Montrealers: when the terrace opens, spring has definitely sprung. The kitchen specializes in crêpes; a few pastas and pizzas are also offered.

Hours: Mon.–Fri. 11:30 a.m.–2 a.m.;
Sat. and Sun. 10 a.m.–2 a.m., May through September

---

407 Place Jacques-Cartier (@ St-Paul)
(514) 861-5731
Metro: Champ-de-Mars

Le Ste-Elisabeth

Thanks to its hidden location on a tiny street just off Ste-Catherine, the Ste-Elisabeth has maintained a low profile among Montreal bar-hoppers. But it's absolutely worth visiting for its rear courtyard, a square patio surrounded by brick walls covered in an incredible 90-foot vine. Understandably, the terrace gets all the attention, but the interior of the Ste-Elisabeth has its own charms. Winter is almost as fun as summer in this pleasant little pub, thanks to a working fireplace that casts a warm glow on the room. There's a good selection of local and imported beer on tap, as well as tasty sangria. On Les Lundis d'Enfer (Mondays from Hell), you can take advantage of drink specials that will trigger a hangover to last you the rest of the week.

Hours: 3 p.m.–3 a.m. daily

1412 Ste-Elisabeth (@ Ste-Catherine)
(514) 286-4302
Metro: Berri-UQAM

Terrasse Magnétique

If you're stuck in the city all summer, an evening at the rooftop bar of Hôtel de la Montagne just might be the vacation you didn't have. This twentieth-floor open-air hideaway, called Terrasse Magnétique, is open to hotel guests and drop-in visitors alike. It offers views of the downtown skyline, tables set beneath little gazebos, and drinks served from cabanas just steps from the pool. Light meals are available, and live music wafts through the air on weekends. On your way up, stop for a cocktail in the hotel lobby's piano bar, which is an ode to Art Deco, complete with gold nymph statues, massive chandeliers, and architectural details that twist and turn into amazing organic shapes. A passageway connects the piano bar to Thursday's, a bar on Crescent.

Hours: 11:30 a.m.–3 a.m., mid-May through Labour Day

1430 de la Montagne (@ de Maisonneuve W.)
(514) 281-5656
Metro: Peel

Tokyo

The Japanese motif outside should give you some hint about the Asian stylings that await you inside the ultra-designed Tokyo. The interior is divided into two rooms: one has a red scheme, the other blue. Among the Zen-chic touches is a recessed seating area that looks like a white-leather whirlpool, only without the water. Live concerts and turntables keep the masses happy with house, R&B, hip-hop, and eighties grooves. On weekends, Tokyo fills up fast with a well-groomed and fun-loving crowd in their mid-twenties, so expect lineups. In warm weather, you can double your fun here with two terraces. The small space at the back feels vaguely like a *Gilligan's Island* set, with its benches and little cabana bar; the rooftop patio, one level above, provides great views of the Plateau.

Hours: Wed. and Fri.–Sun. 10 p.m.–3 a.m.;
Thurs. 5 p.m.–3 a.m.

3709 St-Laurent (@ Pine)
(514) 842-6838
Metro: St-Laurent or Sherbrooke

Alphabetical Index

EATING

DRINKING

Area Index

EATING

Chinatown/Quartier Latin
Café Sinonet 170
Camellia Sinensis 172
Chez Gatsé 58
Exos 174
Hoàng Oanh 156
Hong Kong Restaurant 61
Kam Fung 62
Keung Kee 31
La Paryse 46

Côte-des-Neiges/ Ville Mont-Royal/ Ville St-Laurent
L'Abidjanaise 138
Adonis 154
Bahay Kubo 66
Ban Lao Thai 67
La Caverne 82
Chez Benny 93
Duc de Lorraine 164
Le Georgia 85
Gibeau Orange Julep 150
Jamaica Way 141
Jolee 101
Ma's Place 144
Pushap Sweets 38
Rôtisserie Mavi 135
Taquería Sol y Luna 112
Tasty Foods 120

Downtown
Al-Taib 90
Angela Pizzeria 26
Arahova 27
Au Vieil Istanbul 91
Café l'Étranger 50
Café Presto 123
Café Sarajevo 179
Cocktail Hawaii 173
Cuisine Bangkok 68
Le Galeto 130

Le Grand Comptoir 78
Lola Rosa 36
McKibbins Irish Pub 182
Montreal Pool Room 45
Nonya 69
O-Bentò 63
Phayathai 70
Place Milton 23
Rôtisserie Italienne 127

East End
Chez Clo 19
Japanese Tea Garden 175
Jardin Tiki 151

Gay Village
Le Club Sandwich 30
Kilo 165
La Strega 128
Pho Viet 72
Spirite Lounge 39

Little Italy/Villeray
El Amigo 106
Aux Derniers Humains 74
Café International 122
Do-Ré-Mi 149
Elio Ristorante 124
Hoàng Oanh 156
Irazu 109
Melchorita 22
Motta 118
Napoletana 119
Le Petit Alep 95
Pho Pasteur 71
Shaheen 104
Super-Marché Andes 111
William J. Walter 160

Mile End/Outremont
Arahova 27
Au Bec Fin JRR 139
Bilboquet 162
Café Brazil 107

Index by Cuisine

INTERNATIONAL/ FUSION

MIDDLE EAST

NORTH AMERICA

SOUTH AMERICA

SPECIALTY